the Best

the Best

PETER PASSELL
and
LEONARD ROSS

Farrar, Straus and Giroux • *New York*

Library of Congress Cataloging in Publication Data

Passell, Peter.
  The best.

  1. Consumer education.   2.   Curiosities.
I.   Ross, Leonard, joint author.   II.   Title.
TX335.P35   1974   031'.02   73–87697

WARNING:

Prices in this edition of *The Best* were up to date at the time of publication. For further information, see page 46.

the Best

THE BEST AIRLINE FOOD

A miraculous process really, those ritual meals from individual aluminum troughs, far above the clouds in your Whisperjet or Astrojet, Yellowbird or Proud Bird. Why is it impossible for an airline that has managed to avoid a fatal accident for decades to serve a filet mignon that is pink in the middle?

Not only is airline food an insult to taste, but it's an offense against capitalism. Since the Civil Aeronautics Board and the international air cartel have fixed the fares and leg room (as Pan Am puts it, "Money is one thing you shouldn't worry about in choosing an airline"), food is about the only thing left to compete over. Yet all the airlines seem to outdo each other in awfulness: steamed Polynesian chicken with steamed Polynesian raisins on TWA, steamed beef sinew with steamed tomato gruel on United—or is it the other way around? Nothing seems to work out well, whether the airlines' PR departments aim high (Maxim's for Air France, Trader Vic's for United) or low (Mohawk, may it rest in peace, tried Beer and Pizza Flights to Buffalo). And it isn't a matter of not really caring. Air France, for example, operates its own commissaries at Orly and JFK, complete with chefs trained at Michelin-starred restaurants. They figure on spending about twelve dollars

3

for a first-class meal, not counting alcohol or the otherwise superfluous stewardesses on the aircraft.

Fact is, there is virtually no way to serve an edible hot meal in the air. The only heating facility possible on an airplane is an oven for reheating. All food is partially cooked on the ground, frozen, and then defrosted on board. That will finish off the texture and flavor of any airline's dreamland menu; the stuff durable enough to survive is considered unsuitably exotic (curry) or unsuitably lower-middle-class (macaroni and cheese).

Hence the best airline food is the kind that escapes the fire altogether. Who wouldn't trade a Boeuf Wellington à la manière de Boeing for the seafood and rice salad dished up by an anonymous Schiphol Airport caterer to Air France economy-class passengers? Where was it written that only Avianca could manage a cold crab-meat and lobster platter —once a regular feature of the Miami to Bogotá run?

This all may be pre-senile pessimism, but we believe the Golden Age of airline food ended with the settlement of the Great Sandwich War in the late 1950's. Anticipating a period of excess capacity, the International Air Transport Association promulgated stringent rules on airline service frills, lest some of the member carriers be tempted to pass on the economies of jet aircraft to their customers. Tourist-class passengers were to receive only sandwiches on the North Atlantic run. No one, however, took the trouble to define the term precisely, and a number of airlines came up with elaborate interpretations of the rule—rare-roast-beef-garnished-with-fresh-mayonnaise-and-gherkins provided by KLM, for example. Alas, the airlines came back to their senses and reinstituted the cardboard escalope de veau standard within a year.

Maybe if BOAC were to hire Julia Child instead of Robert Morley . . .

THE BEST AMERICAN WINE

Wine is commercially produced in at least thirty states (including New Mexico, Florida, and Kentucky), but only in a half dozen is the product good for more than getting drunk. On occasion a newspaper food editor, embarrassed to recycle the last recipe for leftover ham, will "discover" the wines of Michigan, or Ohio, or Maryland. We recommend following such hardy explorers at a safe distance.

The reasons for this distressing state of affairs are commercial and meteorological. Almost all of the world's great wine grapes are grown in cloudy, temperate belts of land in France or Germany—the Bordeaux area, Burgundy, the valleys of the Rhine and its tributaries. Sunny summers in Italy, Spain, Greece, North Africa, and central California make for enormous crops, but wines lacking acid and backbone.

The Eastern United States faces the other extreme: long harsh winters, the kind that decimate European Vinifera grapes. One grape variety, the Labrusca family—Concords, Catawbas—does survive the cold, and generates huge juice yields to boot. The trouble is, Labrusca grapes all contain a chemical that gives the wine a characteristic "foxy" taste. It makes bad sweet wines and abominable dry wines. A few enterprising Eastern vineyards have tried to overcome the problem by growing French-American hybrids, vines

5

that will stand the winters and put out a lot of juice without the overpowering *goût de Welch's*. The hybrids are
better than Labruscas; better, but not best.

The best places in North America to grow wine grapes
are the coastal valleys of California north of San Francisco.
There the weather more closely resembles that of Burgundy
and Bordeaux: the winters moderate, the summer morn-
ings foggy, the days cool. All the major European grape
varieties are cultivated, along with one—the Zinfandel—of
obscure origin. Californians believe these Napa and Sonoma
Valley varietals are the best wines in the world.

They are wrong. None of the Bordeaux-like red Cabernet
Sauvignons (the most successful California quality wines)
are up to the standard of the top fifty or so classified
growths of the Médoc; the good Pinot Noir varietals do not
compare with *Premier Cru* Burgundies. Examples of the
very best California reds—Beaulieu Vineyards Cabernet
Sauvignon Private Reserve 1964, Mirassou Cabernet 1964
—would most appropriately be matched with *Bourgeois
Cru* Médocs, or a handful of well-made *petit château*
Bordeaux. Really worthy wines, though not Château Latour
or even the second-rate Château Giscours.

The best white American wines are, oddly enough, made
in New York State. New York is the land of Manischewitz;
Catawba is king. But a small vineyard, Dr. Konstantin
Franks's in the Finger Lakes region, produces vintaged red
and white varietals from European Vinifera vines grafted
on tough Pinot roots native to Canada. Franks's best shot,
the Johannisberg Riesling, varies in quality from decent to
the equivalent of excellent estate-bottled Rheingaus; he
prices them accordingly. None of the good doctor's com-

6

petitors has followed his example, though. Vinifera yields are low, and some maintain that the risk of losing vines over the winter is greater than with Labrusca or hybrid grapes. One winery, Dr. Franks's old employer, Gold Seal, cultivates Viniferas, but it is only beginning to bottle wines made from them unblended.

Perhaps the day will come when outstanding American wines reach the highest French standards. But that day will not come soon. The California vineyards are for the most part much larger than their European equivalents, and each winery feels compelled to produce a dozen different wines. Beaulieu makes fifteen, Mirassou at least seventeen. Diversification means that no single wine gets the attention common to classified European growths.

California's vineyards could, of course, specialize, but that would not change another dismal aspect of the economics of the wine business. Great wines are incredibly expensive to make. Vast inputs of labor are necessary at every stage of cultivation; older vines produce better grapes but less juice. Since red wines should be aged five years or more, the cost of holding and storing five years' output must be permanently underwritten.

Americans are certainly willing to pay the price—a couple of small California vineyards charge ten or fifteen dollars per bottle to private customers and never bother to ship to wine stores. This, however, seems a matter of consumer snobbery rather than discrimination. None of the private reserve wines is better than Beaulieu's best. Affluent Europeans are no more sophisticated selectors of wine, but they have the advantage of reasonably accurate classification systems on which to base their snobbery. In short, we doubt that it will ever pay an American winery to do what must be done in order to compete with Château Margaux.

THE BEST BED SHEETS

BSnobbery isn't the only thing that separates the best from Fieldcrest. The sheets you buy at Gimbels are woven from cotton or cotton and polyester fiber with less than 200 threads to the square inch. O.K., but denser weaves, as high as 300 count, mean the fabric will last far longer. The ultimate sheeting cloth is made from linen thread. It lasts longer than any cotton fabric and remains cooler to the touch, since it's more absorbent.

Good linen has almost disappeared, but some of the shops that cater to the carriage trade will find it for you. D. Porthault of New York makes custom linen sheets in any of six hundred designs or a vast range of solid colors. Expect a double-bed set to cost about $400. If you would like to relieve the monotony of a simple pattern with lace or embroidery, figure on multiplying that price several times over.

THE BEST BOOK ACKNOWLEDGMENT

"Tradition requires that I absolve my critics from responsibility for all errors. Although I deeply respect all tradition as a matter of principle, I see no reason to absolve them. If I have committed blunders, one or another of those learned men and women should have noticed; if they did not, then let them share the disgrace. As for my interpretation and bias, the usual disclaimer is unnecessary since no one in his right mind is likely to hold them responsible for either."

—Eugene D. Genovese, *The World the Slaveholders Made*

THE BEST BOOK OF THE BIBLE

There's a wide choice here—in the King James version, thirty-nine books of the Old Testament, twenty-seven of the New, not counting the Apocrypha—all the way from "In the beginning" (Genesis) to "Alpha and Omega, the beginning and the end" (Revelation). In between, as many bests as in an Academy Awards presentation: II Samuel for best film (*David and Bathsheba*); the Gospel According to St. Matthew for best foreign-language film; Ecclesiastes for best song lyric ("Turn! Turn! Turn!") . . .

We can quickly set aside some books as nonstarters—the minor prophets and obscurer epistles. (Quiz question: distinguish between Zephaniah and Zechariah, or between I Timothy and II Timothy.) Perhaps, too, we should rule out books with only one chapter (Obadiah, Jude, etc.) or even those with less than five, as lacking in variety.

Psalms may be the popular favorite: not merely quotable, but singable. However, it's too obvious a choice. Other front-runners might include Exodus—ten plagues and Ten Commandments. (The rest of the Pentateuch pale in comparison: Leviticus, too full of rules for burnt offerings and cleansing of lepers; Numbers, too numerical; Deuteronomy, with too many divers laws and ordinances.) Judges is the best book for the women's movement, with Deborah, Jael, *and* Delilah, whereas Ruth, Judith, and Esther manage only one heroine apiece. There's Isaiah for optimists, Jeremiah for pessimists, and Ezekiel for acid heads and UFO freaks. Samuel and Kings are fun, and so's Acts. Luke's Gospel is human, John's is profound.

I Corinthians has the beautiful chapter 13, about love—but also the unbeautiful chapter 7, about Paul's sexual hangups. In contrast, there's the Song of Solomon, a real maverick. "By night on my bed I sought him whom my soul loveth." Despite attempts to explain it as God's love for mankind, or Christ's for His Church, it remains unconvincing as a religious text, which disqualifies it.

Our best book is Job, which furnishes variety while retaining a structural unity. If not as exciting as Exodus or Acts, it has a dramatic, Faustian scenario and some of the grandest and loveliest poetry in the Bible. It's got the obligatory famous quotes ("The Lord gave, and the Lord hath taken away; blessed be the name of the Lord") and song lyric, or at least aria lyric ("I know that my redeemer liveth"). It presents a view of nature to glad the heart of any ecologist, including a plea for vanishing species like the eagle and the whale. Above all, it sets man firmly in his place in the universe—as the gloss in our copy of the Bible has it: "the Lord . . . convinceth him of ignorance and imbecility." "Where wast thou when I laid the foundations of the earth?" inquires God, providing an unprovable but, to the faithful, acceptable alternative Best Theory of the Origin of the Universe (which see).

C THE BEST CAMERA AT ANY PRICE

Modern expensive cameras are the visions of technology freaks come true, amazingly versatile machinery for the professional, and supertoys for the compulsive amateur.

The most prestigious name in photography is Leica. Leica manufactures three cameras that could be considered the best: the 35 mm. rangefinder models M4 and M5, and the 35 mm. Leicaflex SL. The M series is a magnificent anachronism, the last chic camera, a 35 mm. with a separate rangefinder. What you get with the M4 is the lightest, simplest, toughest, and most versatile of precision-made camera bodies and the finest lenses in the world. Like almost all lenses, the Leica's are made from a half-dozen or more separately ground elements. And as with all expensive lenses, the acceptable grinding tolerances for the Leica elements are small. But as is not the case with any others, the tiny errors of individual elements are catalogued in a computer that is programmed to match sets of elements to minimize total optical error.

What you don't get in the M4 is what made professional photographers switch to single-lens reflex (SLR) cameras in the 1950's. The M5 corrects one of the weaknesses of rangefinder models with a meter that measures light through the camera lens rather than from a point on the camera body. Quite a trick, but one that costs an extra $175, increases the camera weight by ten ounces, and greatly complicates the process of adjusting the camera exposure. Leica's third camera, the Leicaflex SL, is a true SLR. Much heavier and bulkier than the M series models, the SL does almost anything, including taking pictures with a focal-plane shutter at 1/2000 second.

Only one other 35 mm. camera rates comparison with the Leicas—the Nikon F. Nikon is to Leica what Jaguar is to Lotus—solid engineering, good value, but with distinctions of class. Nikon optics may be a shade inferior, though the F dominates the serious camera market because of an endless array of accessories available: the standard two dozen lenses, a unique 180-degree "fisheye" lens, special close-up equipment, super-size film magazines, and even a motor drive to take hundreds of pictures a minute.

But our own choice for the best is the Swedish Hasselblad. On first sight, what is wrong with this SLR hybrid is more obvious than what is right. It is not ideal for work in the field—the bulky, boxlike camera body obviously evolved from studio equipment. It is almost primitive in function compared to the automatic SLR's; film loading is inconvenient; the process of setting up a shot takes twice as long as with a good 35 mm. Moreover, the price of a good lens system to match the body costs about $4,000, triple that of a Leica system.

What is right about the Hasselblad, however, makes up for the inconvenience in any low-pressure situation. First, the negative size, 2¼ inches square, is triple that of a 35 mm. format, providing greater detail with equivalent film. Second, each of the German Zeiss lenses comes with its own shutter system, an awesomely costly luxury that permits the use of flash with any lens up to a shutter speed of 1/5000 second. Third, the film magazines (there is even one for Polaroid film) can be changed in mid-roll; that's far easier than carrying two or three cameras.

These features may not convince even the average professional to buy the Rolls-Royce of cameras, but others on less limited budgets have been sufficiently impressed: NASA regularly sends Hasselblads (and Nikon F's) along with the astronauts.

THE BEST CAMERA UNDER $100

Ferocious competition and a new generation of cheap electronics technology means that $100 buys a lot of camera.

Certainly the most popular cameras in this range are the kind that load film in cartridges and have few controls to confuse or bore the uncommitted amateur. Some, notably the Kodak Pocket Instamatics, provide decent value and ultimate simplicity, but at the cost of photo quality and flexibility. Cartridge cameras have mediocre lenses, slow electronic shutters, and rudimentary rangefinders that virtually limit their use to the casual snapshot.

In theory, one could correct these faults; Kodak has in fact ventured onto the market with an overpriced single-lens reflex Instamatic that meets the minimum criteria of serious photography. But classier optics and a better camera body can't make up for the basic design fault of the cartridges. On a conventionally loaded camera the film is aligned flat on the focal plane by a metal back plate. The film plane of a cartridge cannot be locked in so rigidly. The result: slightly fuzzy negatives no matter how carefully you focus.

If one can make it over the hurdle of threading 35 mm. film into a camera, everything changes for the better. One hundred dollars buys the Japanese Olympus 35SP, a carefully finished, automated rangefinder camera with a very respectable f 1.7, seven-element lens and shutter speeds up to 1/500 second. On automatic, all you do is set the film speed and focus. Electronic circuits translate the light measurement into the appropriate lens aperture and shutter speed. If you are using a flash, the same circuitry will adjust the f stop to compensate for the distance of the subject in focus. A button on the back keys in a spot meter that measures light only from the center of the picture; that's a useful option if you focus into a bright background.

Another 35 mm. rangefinder camera, the Minolta Hi-Matic E, is even more the idiot's delight. But unlike the Olympus SP, it cannot be operated on a manual override of the automatic circuits. Still, the advantages of the Hi-Matic are seductive. Its electronic shutter can open and close in 1/1000 second. If you attach a specially mated electronic flash, the Minolta will automatically switch it on when the light level is too low for flashless shooting.

The major differences between these $100 compacts and more expensive 35's are accuracy and flexibility. The optics are good but not great, the light meter adequate but not as reliable as the behind-the-lens variety. And most important, there are no provisions for interchangeable lenses. For about $30 more, the single-lens reflex Olympus Pen FT offers additional features with only a minor sacrifice in automaticity: behind-the-lens metering and viewing, a choice of specialized interchangeable lenses. The only serious drawback is the feature that permits the FT to take up so little space. The FT uses 35 mm. film, one half of a frame at a time. That means economy in film use, but smaller negatives that lose detail in enlargement, particularly as color slides.

THE BEST CHAMPAGNE

Champagne violates all the rules. Rugged individualism reigns in most wine regions of France, but the Champagne country is organized enough to make any New Dealer proud. A fine Bordeaux is the product of grapes from a single vintage grown within the boundaries of a single estate and is invariably bottled within sight of the vines. Champagne has no châteaux, just privately owned fields, and factories in the cellars of nearby towns. Leaving nothing to chance, grape prices are negotiated annually by committees of notables, virtually the entire crop going to the twenty or so major shippers. Good (and bad) champagnes are blends of different grapes and different harvests, no more associated with a unique place or time than the family Buick.

What this arrangement loses in romanticism it gains in simplicity. You can choose champagne by brand like gin. Year-to-year variations in the quality of the harvest are pretty well evened out by varying the blend and adding sugar or acid. The big exporters like Moët & Chandon aim for a uniform product—if you liked it last year, you'll like it next.

This is not to suggest that all champagne is the same. When shippers believe they have unusually good grapes, they limit the amount of blending with wine from other years and label the bottles by vintage. Vintage champagnes, however, are not always better than their anonymous siblings; the commercial pressure to declare a vintage year is substantial, especially when it is possible to bask in the reflected glory of great vintages from other wine regions. Of the vintages now available, 1966 is probably the best—unlike still white wines, good champagne can endure, perhaps improve, in the bottle for a decade or more.

Vintage champagnes are usually sold as "*brut*," a term that refers to the amount of sugar added to the bottle. In general, the less sugar, the better the champagne. Sugar has to be used to flesh out a bad year; its absence suggests the shipper has nothing to hide. However, *brut*, the least sweet category, has no precise definition. All that stops a producer from calling everything *brut* is the frail constraints of reputation.

Very expensive champagne often carries the label *Blanc de Blancs* or *Tête de Cuvée*. Neither is an absolute guar-

16

antee of quality. *Blanc de Blancs* means the champagne was fermented entirely from Chardonnay grapes, rather than from a mixture of Chardonnay and Pinot Noir. There is certainly nothing wrong with Pinot Noir—it is the rock upon which all great red Burgundies are built. But Chardonnay grapes do produce a paler, more delicate wine that is *à la mode*. *Tête de Cuvée* is champagne made the standard way from the first pressing of the grapes. Whether the pressing matters much is debatable; the mark really implies that it is the top of the shipper's line. Among the *Tête de Cuvée* seen in the United States, Dom Pérignon from Moët & Chandon is the most popular. We prefer a good vintage by Louis Roederer or Pol Roger, the best of the export houses.

Short of the best—which some may find an extravagance at twenty dollars—it doesn't make much sense to buy champagne. The twelve-dollar variety is rarely worth the price, since competitive alternatives can be had for half as much. From France, the dry sparkling wines of Seyssel are often the equal of medium-priced champagne. California "champagne" (the long arm of French labeling law does not reach across the Atlantic) can also be quite decent; the best are Korbel Natural and Hans Kornell.

THE BEST CHESS PLAYER OTHER THAN BOBBY FISCHER

Fischer dominates the game. Who's second best is less clear.

None of the other Americans, with the possible exceptions of Sammy Reshevsky and Robert Byrne, plays world championship chess. Reshevsky was eight times the national champion and owned U.S. chess until Fischer came along. He's too old to get better. Byrne only recently showed the capacity to beat really fine players, but he did very well in the candidates' tournament for the next cycle of world championship matches. Few would give him the slightest chance of topping the best three or four international grandmasters; the day still might come.

That leaves the Russians, the once and future kings of chess. Among them, romantics gravitate to Mikhail Tal, the world champion for a single year in the early sixties, winning and then losing with Botvinnik. A decade ago Tal played the most exciting games of modern history, always on the attack, snatching victory from sacrifices that first appeared to be blunders. In contrast, Fischer's style is positively middle-aged: fine, if unflashy, attack ability combined with an encyclopedic understanding of the position game. After his fall, Tal never sustained his diabolical abilities long enough to win a crucial match, though in the last year or two he has toned down his style and produced some big wins. He will not get a chance to meet Fischer soon, however, since he chose the candidates' tournament for one of his periodic collapses.

Ironically, the youngest star of Soviet chess is everything Tal was not. A percentage player content to wait and squeeze out points, Anatoli Karpov belongs to the school of the former world champion Petrosian. Unlike Petrosian, he makes mistakes.

That leaves Boris Spassky. Since the humiliation in Iceland, critics have forgotten how good Spassky is. It's true he was smashed in the first half-dozen games, but from the mid-point of the series the Soviet champion was nearly

Fischer's equal. Spassky came across in the press as a diffident conservative, a nice guy, but no competition for the enfant terrible. In fact, his style shows the same balance as Fischer's: strong offense, fine positional play. That Spassky is not as good as Fischer doesn't mean that he isn't better than everyone else.

THE BEST CHOCOLATE MOUSSE

SUSAN PREVIANT LEE'S CHOCOLATE MOUSSE:

- 6 tablespoons strong coffee
- 4 tablespoons cognac
- 8 ounces semisweet chocolate
- ¼ cup superfine sugar
- 1¾ to 2 cups heavy cream
- 1 tablespoon superfine sugar
- ¼ teaspoon vanilla

Pour coffee and cognac into a double boiler. Add chocolate and heat. After chocolate is melted, stir until the mixture is well blended. Add sugar, and continue stirring over heat until mixture is glossy. Let mixture cool.

Make crème chantilly by whipping heavy cream until very thick. Beat sugar and vanilla into cream. With a rubber spatula, slowly and thoroughly blend chocolate mixture into cream.

Cover and refrigerate. *Serves six.*

THE BEST CIGAR

The finest cigars are made in Havana, the H. Upmann (John Kennedy's favorite) and the Montecristo, the brands of choice. Politics has had little impact on the quality of the Cuban product, at least according to smokers in Europe and Canada, whose governments permit the importation of Communist weed. Since cigars age well—indeed, they benefit from a few years of storage under controlled humidity —pre-Castro Havanas are still available in the United States, though at prohibitive prices.

A legal alternative to the real thing is the Montecruz, a luxury cigar manufactured in the Canary Islands by the former owners of the nationalized H. Upmann factory. Whether the Montecruz, or other expensive cigars made in Jamaica, Honduras, or Florida, can meet the standards of a true Havana is a matter of dispute. As in the case of the elite of German and French wines, the quality of cigar tobacco is tied to the soil. Château Lafite-Rothschild could not be made from grapes grown in California or, for that matter, from grapes grown in any other vineyard in the village of Pauillac. But the analogy can be pushed too far. Unlike great wines, the finest cigars are made from blends of raw materials, not from the output of single estates. While the best filler tobacco (the bulk of the cigar) comes from Cuba, Central American substitutes can be very good. Besides, the best cigar wrappers, the thin, virtually non-aromatic leaves that encase the filler and internal binder leaf, come from Sumatra, Connecticut, and the Cameroons.

THE BEST COGNAC

If you distill wine made from grapes, the result is brandy. If the wine happens to be the sour white wine of the St.-Emilion grape grown in the French departments of Charente and Charente-Maritime, the brandy is cognac.

Actually, much more than distillation is required to transform the vulgar Charente wines into the most elegant of brandies. Colorless, freshly brewed cognac must be aged in wooden barrels—not any wooden barrels, but ones fashioned from Limousin oak that has been weathered about five years. The Limousin oak is extremely scarce, particularly the preferred lumber from trees eighty to one hundred years old. The search, however, for acceptable substitutes has been fruitless.

How long the cognac stays in the barrel determines its color (the longer, the darker) and, to a degree, its quality. To be labeled for export as V.S.O.P. (Very Special Old Pale), cognac must be at least four years old. No official attempt to keep track of cognac past five years is made. Hence the credibility of claims depends on the credibility of the shipper, though undoubtedly a large portion of V.S.O.P.'s do spend ten years or more in the barrel. Lesser cognacs, always a minimum of two years old, are commonly called Three-Star.

Charente has some seven thousand distillers, large and small, who produce cognac. All cognacs that leave the region, however, are blends; it is the only way to produce a uniform taste from vintage to vintage. The best blends come from the district of Cognac, the so-called Grande Champagne (why "champagne" is obscure); the next best from Petite Champagne, nearby. A mix of these two will be labeled Fine Champagne.

Barrel age—once brandy is bottled, time cannot improve it—and locality are the determining factors of quality. But there is still too much room to maneuver within the law to be able to infer quality simply from a label. Thus Otard's Three-Star is better than some V.S.O.P. Grande Champagne.

In short, the only guarantee of superior cognac is the name of the shipper. Under twenty dollars, Rémy Martin's Fine Champagne is an excellent compromise between extremes of delicacy and richness. Hennessy markets a grade above its V.S.O.P. that is not surpassed among standard export cognacs—the price, alas, was last seen at thirty dollars and climbing.

Armagnac, the brandy of southwest France, has the decided advantage over cognac of costing much less. While some is sold in France in its uncivilized adolescence, the armagnac that reaches alien shores is in general quite good.

It can never be as delicate as a light-bodied cognac, but delicacy is a lesser virtue of brandy. Armagnac benefits from aging as much as cognac; old armagnac has the same controlled energy, the same dark fire. And unlike the situation with cognac, the commercial temptation to blend and bottle young is apparently not overwhelming.

THE BEST COLLEGE AT OXFORD

Magdalen, both the most beautiful and the most intellectually diverse. Christ Church is an unreconstructed sanctuary of the worst in British snobbery; Balliol is like an American law school, full of politics and ambition. Magdalen has everything: class warfare on even terms, superb tutors, an immense spectrum of interests and tastes.

THE BEST CON GAME

In its romantic form, the con game is a celebration of individual initiative over mass cupidity. A classic con need not even be blatantly illegal. Consider Golden Potato, in which the artist offers a solid-gold potato to the person who sends him the largest number of the ordinary kind. Or this more complex game described by A. J. Leibling:

Pick a single horse race a few days in advance, say the first at Belmont next Saturday, with seven horses entered.

23

Then choose seventy names at random from the phone book, call each one, and explain that you know the winner of the first at Belmont next Saturday. Name a horse, changing the choice every tenth phone call, so that, no matter which horse wins, ten people will think you picked correctly. Then call up those ten and "pick" yet another race, covering all possible winners. Now call up the lucky person a third time—there has to be at least one—but this round *sell* the name of the winner of a future race . . .

Irresistible though the individualist tradition may be— George C. Scott or Burt Lancaster in top hat and tails with snake oil in hand—the real con money lies in corporate finance. Two hundred and fifty years ago, at the height of the South Sea Bubble speculations, one consortium successfully floated stock "for an undertaking which shall in due time be revealed." But the spectacular modern con awaited the evolution of the corporate conglomerate in which all manner of hanky-panky could be drowned in a sea of bureaucracy and computer printout.

The Equity Funding Corporation went public in 1964 with the clever notion of peddling life insurance and mutual funds as a package. The idea was to allow customers to pay the premiums on the insurance by borrowing from Equity, with the mutual fund shares as collateral. If the fund had a good track record, its earnings could eventually pay off the loans with interest. Quite a deal: "free" insurance plus a mutual fund nest egg.

To this legal sleight of hand for the customers, the press has reported that Equity Funding added some illegal sleight of hand for its stockholders. Stock prices reflect earnings and, more important, anticipated earnings. Equity gave the market plenty to anticipate by hyping its profits in two ways. The first and less aesthetic con was making out-and-out fraudulent balance-sheet reports. In 1972 Equity claimed $77 million in loans due from its customers as assets of the company—about half the entire stockholders' equity—loans that didn't exist. Another $32 million in reported assets consisted of bonds and commercial paper —that also didn't exist.

The more original side of the con (anybody can lie to an auditor) was the bogus sale of Equity's policies to other life insurance companies. Selling policies is a common practice in the industry; the seller exchanges the right to collect future premiums for cash on the barrelhead—as much as 190 percent of the first year's premium. But Equity's practice was far from common. It created policies never actually written and kept a staff busy eight hours a day forging the necessary medical forms. Equity was in effect selling a chain letter—but with a catch. To keep last year's phony policies from being discovered this year, cash had to be found to pay this year's premiums. The only way to get the cash was to sell still more phony policies that would have to be serviced in the future—an ever-expanding pyramid of policies that within a decade would have required Equity to claim more policies in force than all other insurance companies in the world, combined.

It is this suicidal aspect to Equity's deception that disqualifies it. What is the point of a con in which there is no way to escape with the loot? Besides, Equity's high jinks can't compare with Robert Vesco's rape of Investor's Overseas Services, a corporate body already soiled by one major fraud. IOS was a collection of mutual funds based outside the United States by its founder Bernie Cornfeld to avoid all those silly little SEC and IRS rules. During the hiatus after Cornfeld's manipulations of the billion-dollar funds were discovered, IOS was virtually leaderless. Best yet, the directors seemed to understand little about the complex corporate structure Cornfeld had erected.

Vesco gained command of IOS in August 1970 simply by lending it a supposedly needed $5 million, which he in turn borrowed from a little bank in the Bahamas. Once chairman of the IOS finance committee, Vesco deposited $5 million IOS cash in the same bank—in effect Vesco took over without risking a penny. Vesco's only rival on the IOS board was Cornfeld. No problem here—Vesco arranged to buy out Cornfeld's six million shares with $5.5 million in IOS funds. Less than a year later, IOS (Vesco) transferred the same block of stock to Vesco for $50,000.

That set the stage for the big coup. While fending off Swiss legal authorities with—allegedly—a helping hand from John Mitchell, IOS purchased a number of Bahamas-based empty corporate shells owned by Vesco and associates. In return Vesco received substantial percentages of IOS stock. As if this were not enough, one of Vesco's companies received an additional six-million-share thank-you from IOS in consideration for the original $5 million "emergency" loan. By the time the SEC got excited enough to close down the U.S. part of the operation, Vesco and friends had gutted IOS for an estimated $225 million, $110 million of which disappeared utterly without a trace.

THE BEST CORPORATE RESPONSIBILITY
ACHIEVEMENT

Standard Oil of California planned to disguise its Scottish
petrochemical complex as a medieval castle. Drawbridge
and moat proved insufficient lure, however, for local residents; the proposal was vetoed.

THE BEST CRUISE SHIP

Two decades ago, the best cruise ships were craft specially
built for that purpose. The big transatlantic liners were
used off-season for cruising, but the afterthought quality of
the idea showed up in space set aside for long-haul pro-
visions and clumsy conversions to single-class sailing.

Not so today. Transatlantic service is dying—there just
aren't enough people who want to spend $400 and five days
in uncertain weather to cross the ocean—and the new ships
have all been designed to maximize the comfort of the
passengers who bring in the profits.

The best of these is the *France*. The 66,000-ton ship is a
luxurious, if cramped, resort hotel with a dining room once
called by Craig Claiborne the best French restaurant in the
world. It surely isn't (unless perhaps you identify yourself
as the food editor of *The New York Times*), but the kitchen
is very good. Almost anything is available for the asking,
and the wine list includes a dramatic collection of rare
vintages at one third the price you would pay in New York.
The sheer size of the *France* means extraordinary variety

27

and comforts: an honest library, a twenty-four-hour bar, gymnasium, substantial boutique, as well as the usual swimming pools and movie theater.

The only real question about cruising on the *France* is why cruise at all. It's nice to be pampered and eat all you want and never have to worry about speaking the language or finding a taxi, one supposes. But for the price of a good cruise you could spend equal time on a beach in Morocco or at the Hotel Crillon in Paris, with less risk to your waistline and heart, and without the chance of boring tablemates or seasickness.

THE BEST DEAL

DFor a Roman slave, teaching Greek; in the Middle Ages, clipping coins; in the nineteenth century, selling rifles to the Union army; in our own age, running a broadcast station. Radio licenses, to those who got there first, cost nothing: quickly they were worth a mint. As early as 1926, a radio station whose apparatus was worth $200,000 was sold for $1,000,000. When television came along, the F.C.C. adopted a straightforward policy: if you had made a small fortune off a free radio license, you were presumed qualified to make a large fortune off a free television license. More rigorous qualifications are required for getting a cable TV franchise: since the F.C.C. isn't involved, you had better know a councilman.

THE BEST-DEFINED JOB IN GOVERNMENT

Administrative Assistant to the Assistant Administrator for Administration, Agency for International Development.

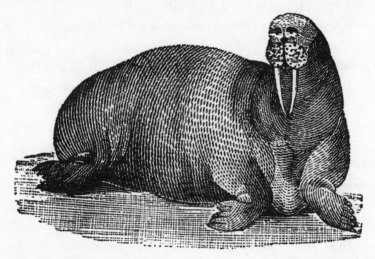

THE BEST DIET

The crashing bore of it all. Everybody knows what the best diet is: the one in the junior high textbook *Personality and Good Health*, right after the chapter on why you shouldn't get carried away on the first date. Lean meat, cottage cheese, skim milk, an occasional slice of bread or a baked potato, fresh fruit and vegies; no skipping breakfast, apples and carrot sticks for snacks, plenty of leafy greens to prevent the inevitable. In case your reading skills aren't up to par, pastel color pictures of lean meat, cottage cheese, etc., are thoughtfully provided. Charts showing ideal weights by height and sex, calorie equivalents of common (the word requires emphasis) foods, and recommended calorie intakes come tacked on at the end. The only thing wrong with the diet—besides the fact that no one in his right mind would stick to it—is that the calorie recommendations are too generous, even for the intended audience.

What of the painless diets written by genuine M.D.'s that cost only $7.95 hardback? They work too—but there is a catch. For practical purposes, nothing counts but calories. A pound of fat contains 3,500 calories. Metabolize 500 a day more than you eat, and you lose a pound a week, give or take a bit. Water makes up the difference, either way. When it doesn't work, one of two things is happening: you are cheating (an eight-ounce hamburger has *twice* as many cals as a four-ounce hamburger) or you are one of many unfortunates able to subsist on the rice ration of a Vietnamese refugee.

How, then, is it possible to lose weight on all the pistachios you can eat, or the four-martini lunch? Because 2,000 calories' worth of pistachios is a lot of pistachios—a pound and a half of the kind in the shells. There is a good chance you'll lose your appetite chowing down a single food before you top your daily allowance. Add an initial weight loss due to dehydration—a common side effect of dramatic changes in food intake—and that accounts for the success of exotic diets.

So far, so good. If a pound and a half of pistachios is more satisfying than the lean meat and baked potato route, what's the problem? There are really only two kinds of these diets—the high-fat, low-carbohydrate version (Dr. Atkins'; Calories Don't Count) and the low-protein, low-fat version (Rice Diet, Drinking Man's Diet, Rockefeller Diet). Neither will put you in the hospital right away—unless you happen to be diabetic—but both are dangerous, certainly if you keep at it for any length of time. A high-fat diet almost always means a diet high in saturated fats: meat, cheese, butter, ice cream. You would have to be illiterate these days not to know that lapping up fat raises cholesterol levels in the blood. And while it is not certain that elevated blood cholesterol leads to heart attacks, it's likely. Metabolizing a high-fat diet in the absence of carbohydrates also leads to changes in blood chemistry—Dr. Atkins' famous ketosis—as well as retention of uric acid. Nothing to worry about for a few weeks, but over the long haul it may be the *coup de grasse* for your kidneys.

Low-fat diets—all the brown rice and/or gin you can swill—are protein deficient. No way to build strong muscles and bones twelve ways. Less obvious is the damage done by heavy carbo intake. For incipient diabetics—a large fraction of the indulgent middle-aged—direct sugar doses will force the diabetes out of the closet. Sugar may also play a role (what doesn't?) in heart disease. The controversy over what causes cholesterol build-up in the arteries is in a state of flux. What is known, however, is that rapid increases in blood sugar call forth insulin output, which in turn seems to have something to do with the synthesis of cholesterol.

No matter what diet you may try, the odds are it won't

31

work, or if it does work, it won't for long. Sticking to the kind of diet that will change your average fat person into a skinny one is a very painful experience. Most of the people who take it off and keep it off do so only after a heart attack, or high-blood-pressure diagnosis, or diabetes—in other words, they are incredibly frightened. The preachy-respectable nutritionists nobody listens to are quick to blame eating habits, and they may be right. Obviously heredity also plays some part—or are all those farmers breeding fat bulls with fat cows just fools?

But "why" is beside the point. The species is flawed, and perfection apparently does not lie in half-time pep talks or hours logged on the analyst's couch. A more promising approach is figuring out how appetite works and controlling it with drugs. Even compulsive overeating is vulnerable to such attacks—amphetamines, for example, knock out the most determined appetite but are obviously not a practical solution in the long run. That does not mean less disruptive chemical weapons will not be found to do the same job.

Since that happy day is distant, the reader may wish to consider the Turner Diet, named after one Shirley Turner of Nottingham, England. Ms. Turner has had her jaw surgically wired shut, leaving only enough room for a straw.

THE BEST DOOR LOCK

There is no point to installing an expensive, pick-resistant lock in a door that can be easily jimmied. Most burglars know nothing of the art of lock-picking. And the few who do are unwilling to risk the minutes of exposure necessary to pick a moderately complicated cylinder for the prospect two television sets and a Boehm sculpture. Hence the primary deterrent against burglary is a solid wood or steel door with a snug steel frame. A protective metal sheath on the frame opposite the lock also makes sense.

By the same logic, the capacity of the lock to absorb punishment is more important than the pick resistance of the lock cylinder. Doorknob locks are the lowliest of defenses—once the knob has been broken off with a pipe wrench, a child can finish the job. A good mortise lock—the kind with a bolt independent of the knob—can't be so easily attacked with burglars' tools. First, the bolt will not be spring-loaded, thereby preventing entry by means of a celluloid strip or credit card. Second, the bolt will extend well into the doorframe to prevent jimmying with a crowbar or spreading tool. The best lock body (they cost $40 to $100 installed) is probably the Segal or the Arrow. The Arrow's bolt is a full inch long, about twice that of the average lock mechanism.

A good lock cylinder must be difficult to pick and should have keys that are difficult to duplicate. The most popular and most pick-proof of the high-security cylinders is the Medeco. While cylinder locks differ in details, the principle is always the same. Inside, the cylinder is prevented from rotating by spring-loaded metal pins that extend into the lock body. When the proper key is inserted, the pins are displaced upward just enough so that they disengage the cylinder. A professional could not hope to defeat the mechanism in the Medeco in less than two hours.

If the major security threat is key duplication rather than picking, the Sargent Keso model will be best. No locksmith has the equipment to make a Keso key; replacements must be obtained by application to the factory. Medeco's duplication system is less direct—the keys must be cut on high-technology machinery sold only to Medeco-licensed dealers.

Even a high-quality cylinder may end up the weakest link. Some cylinders can be destroyed with a screwdriver and hammer far more easily than they can be picked. The ones that require a tubular-type key blank like the Ace are, however, least vulnerable to abuse.

Using much more than a good lock and cylinder may be counterproductive in cities where street crime is as much to be feared as burglary. Auxiliary locks or special devices like the Magic Eye brace lock (better known as the police lock) certainly increase the time it takes a burglar to force the door. But they also increase the chance of being mugged while you fumble with the keys. Door chains provide only a false sense of security—they are a cinch to snap once the door is open.

E THE BEST ELECTRONIC POCKET CALCULATOR

Apart from their conventional virtues, electronic pocket calculators make marvelous adult toys. And with a little creative accounting they can even be written off at tax time. If a toy is all you are really looking for, there's no need to spend more than forty or fifty dollars for a Casio, Rapidman, or one of a half-dozen others. Thanks to the miracles of large-scale integrated circuitry and underpaid Asian labor, that amount buys a reasonably dependable machine that adds, subtracts, multiplies, and divides faster than the eye can see. Plenty good enough to balance a checkbook, or compare the value of 6 ounces of A&P Eight O'Clock Instant Coffee at 95¢ with 8 ounces of Pathmark Freeze Dried at $1.57.

Serious consumer types will detect some differences on the next steps up. Twenty dollars more gets you eight digits of bright red or blue display instead of six, a battery recharger/AC current converter, perhaps a key to lock in a constant for multiplying and dividing. Unlike most of the competition, Sharp's mini also remembers the last number, nice for serial calculations like $(4 + 5)$ divided by $(3 + 2)$. Texas Instruments' cheap model features algebraic rather than arithmetic logic, jargon for the convenient method of punching in the signs in the sequence you would write them.

Go to $100 and the choice becomes interesting:

—The Canon Pocketronic, the only pocket calculator (you would need a very large pocket) that prints the answers instead of flashing them on a screen. This lets you

35

check the calculation, absolutely vital for adding long columns of figures. And very sexy, if technology turns you on; the printing mechanism is quite unconventional.

—The Texas Instruments SR-10 takes square roots and reciprocals. It also automatically displays numbers too big to fit on the eight-digit register in scientific notation.

—The Sinclair Executive doesn't do anything special, but looks great. It is super-thin (⅜″), jet black, a perfect rectangular solid with a minimum of interruptions . . . the Mies van der Rohe to everybody else's supermarket modern.

But the ultimate pocket calculators are something very different, premonitions of a future invented by Arthur Clarke. The Hewlett-Packard 45 is 6″ × 3″ × 1″ and weighs nine ounces. Yet (besides the ordinary things) it can remember fourteen ten-digit numbers at once, calculate trigonometric functions, common and natural logarithms, exponentials, factorials, means, standard deviations, convert rectangular coordinates to polar and English measures to metric. All that button-pushing slow you down? The HP-65 can be programmed via magnetic tape cards to compute dozens of complicated operations in sequence. A business version, the HP-80, figures bond yields, sum-of-the-digits depreciations, the present value of fixed-income securities, and projects trend lines with linear regressions. The model 80 also has a built-in 200-year calendar that can tell you what day of the week August 7, 2082, will fall on, or how many days have passed since May 8, 1919.

Of course, just why you would want to know how many days have passed since May 8, 1919, is one problem Hewlett-Packard can't solve.

THE BEST ESTIMATE OF THE DATE OF
THE NEXT ICE AGE

Seventeen thousand years ago, at the peak of the Great Ice
Age, glaciers a mile or two thick extended as far south as
St. Louis—all told, about 30 percent of the earth was
covered. The permanent snows, of course, haven't been
around for a while—Maine saw its last glacier around 3000
B.C.—and all that's left to show for the ice is a remodeled
geography (the Great Lakes, etc.) and a lot of water (the
oceans are three hundred feet deeper).

Skiers, don't abandon hope. Winters are getting colder
and summers milder once again. The polar icecap has ex-
panded a bit over the last thirty years and ecologists claim
to have spotted changes in the migratory habits of animals
sensitive to cold. This isn't the first time in recorded history
that the climate has fluctuated, of course. During the
Middle Ages, centuries of mild winters permitted land-poor
Westerners to push onto the previously inhospitable plains
of Eastern Europe. Greenland, now 80 percent engulfed by
permafrost, became warm enough to support Scandinavian
settlers. However, the weather turned for the worse in the
sixteenth century and did not show signs of recovery until
about 1900.

What, then, makes the recent cooling so ominous? Probably nothing. By the record of the last thousand years, the
worst we are in for is an occasional crop failure in Canada
or Russia, some nasty April blizzards, and a touch more

37

ransom for the oil sheiks. But if you don't have enough to worry about, here's something to grab onto. Along with short weather cycles—a few centuries each—there seem to be much longer cycles. The last long warm spell between ice ages lasted about ten thousand years, and by that reckoning, we're due. When the real thing does come along, we can't expect much warning. It took only a century to make the transition from temperate to subarctic last time around.

Speculation would be unnecessary if we knew why the climate changed in the first place. Some people have toyed with theories about self-generating cycles in wind and air currents, but the most appealing explanation is the simplest —the earth's share of solar energy probably fluctuates. It may be the sun is waxing and waning for reasons of its own; a change of only seven or eight degrees would make much of the earth uninhabitable. A more devious possibility is that the earth wobbles a little in orbit, enough to upset the seasonal distribution of solar energy, which could in turn trigger growth of the icecaps.

On top of all that, changes in the earth's atmosphere could make a difference. Dust in the air shields the earth from the sun—big volcanic eruptions in the South Pacific in 1815 may explain the June frosts of 1816. Burning fossil fuels has the opposite effect, since the resulting carbon dioxide reduces the capacity of the earth to radiate heat back into space. For all we know, Reddi-Kilowatt and the Exxon tiger stand between us and cold times.

THE BEST ESTIMATE OF THE NUMBER OF ANGELS IN THE UNIVERSE

301,655,722, according to a group of fourteenth-century cabalists who employed the device of "calculating words into numbers and numbers into words"—the inspiration, no doubt, for the formula used to apportion federal revenue-sharing funds.

THE BEST ESTIMATE OF WORLD POPULATION IN THE YEAR 2100

The population of the world increased about 2.6 percent a year in the past decade. That doesn't sound so bad until one remembers the miracles of compound interest—people's children have children, who have more children. Simply projecting the 2.6 percent rate of increase, the world's population would double every thirty years and reach 83 billion by the beginning of the twenty-second century.

But such projections are probably misleadingly pessimistic. The population explosion is a modern phenomenon, largely the result of improvements in public health in the past few centuries. Before, most countries maintained stable populations by balancing high birth rates with high death rates. DDT, urban sewage systems, and improved emergency food distribution cut the rate of slaughter but left fertility unaffected.

Luckily, social forces may counteract this natural discrepancy between reproduction and death. In Western Europe, the USSR, Japan, and North America, birth rates have fallen to match mortality rates—population growth continues in the United States only because of the "bulge" of young people born during the baby boom of the forties and fifties. No one really knows why birth rates have fallen —or, indeed, that large families won't become fashionable once again. But it is easy to speculate. First, birth-control technology gives people a more acceptable way of limiting family size. The Irish achieved the same goal long ago, but only by pushing the age of marriage to nearly thirty. Perhaps as important, children have become sort of a luxury. In a rural society extra mouths to feed don't cost much and, besides, the kids can be put to work at an early age. But in the city, children cost more and are dependent longer. Also, as wages go up, the implied cost of keeping mothers out of the labor force increases.

For most of the developed countries, the period of adjustment—the time between the fall in death rates and the fall in birth rates—took at least a century. Today the process seems to be working much more rapidly; demographers argue that India and other parts of Asia are already experiencing declining birth rates.

If worldwide reproduction rates decline to just the level needed to maintain a constant population by the year 2000, the planet will top off at eight and a half billion; if it takes an extra forty years, population will reach a rather cozy sixteen billion.

THE BEST EVIDENCE OF LIFE ON
OTHER PLANETS

If most other star systems resemble our own—there's every reason to believe they do—there exist in the universe about one billion billion planets that could support life. Trouble is, they are so far away it's almost impossible to find out for certain that we have company. No planet outside the solar system has ever been observed; we only know they are there at all from the gravitational pull they exert on their stars.

A really advanced extraterrestrial civilization might, of course, try to contact us—quite a feat of technology, but then, we have only ourselves for comparison. Intrigued by the possibility, astronomers have been listening for intelligent radio signals for the last fifteen years. In 1968 it looked as if the search was paying off. The Cambridge University observatory discovered pulsars, powerful radio sources broadcasting uniform bursts of energy so regular they could be used as super-accurate clocks. Pulsars turn out to be stars smaller than the earth, yet as much as ten billion times as bright as the sun. Alas, there is a natural explanation for these miniature sentinels of the universe, and though it can't be proven that some incredible civilization isn't at the controls, it doesn't seem likely.

The next best thing to communication with another star would be evidence of life within the solar system. Meteorites, probably the debris of disintegrated planets, often contain traces of complex carbon molecules. These molecules are not fossils—crucial ingredients are missing—but

41

they might be the suitable building material for life in hospitable environments.

None of the other planets really qualifies as hospitable, though there is a good chance Mars could support life and a long-shot case to be made for Venus and Jupiter. By any standard, Mars is no paradise. There is only a trace of oxygen in the atmosphere, probably little water (the polar regions seem to be covered with dry ice), and the temperatures fall well below zero every night. Primitive life, however, can be quite tough. *Streptococcus mitis* bacteria left on the moon by *Surveyor III* were still alive three years later. Several earthly organisms can reproduce at thirty degrees below zero, and some plants can make it through nights of Martian-like temperatures in Martian-like, oxygen-poor atmospheres.

Life on Mars—nothing too fancy, of course—would also explain the seasonal color changes in the planet's dark regions, as well as the puzzlingly rapid recovery of colors after what are assumed to be dust storms. Vegetation on the order of lichen has been suggested, but a much hardier version than the ordinary scaly stuff you find on rocks. The Russian and American Mars probes, scheduled for the mid-seventies when the earth passes close by, may settle the issue.

THE BEST EVIDENCE THAT IRONY WAS
NOT INVENTED BY OSCAR WILDE

When asked to comment on a scheme to unite the Continent as a step toward perfect government, Frederick the Great of Prussia replied that it was "a capital notion requiring merely the assent of the Crowned Heads of Europe for its adoption."

THE BEST EVIDENCE THAT TIMES
HAVE CHANGED

Life magazine's December 22, 1941, issue features a handy pictorial guide on "How to Tell Japs from the Chinese," a problem few Americans had faced until two weeks earlier. The average Chinese, according to *Life*, has a "lanky, lithe build," with a "long and delicately boned" face, while "Japs . . . betray aboriginal antecedents in a squat, long-torsoed build, a broader, more massively boned head and face, flat, often pug, nose, yellow-ocher skin and heavier beard."

Such distinctions can be tricky to discern, *Life* confesses: Chinese, "when middle-aged and fat . . . look more like Japs . . . An often sounder clue is facial expression, shaped by cultural, not anthropological, factors. Chinese wear rational calm of tolerant realists. Japs, like General Tojo, show humorless intensity of ruthless mystics."

THE BEST EXAMPLE OF ANALYTIC THOUGHT

"Whenever a person is called upon to make a speech, the first question that enters his mind is 'What shall I talk about?' "

—Gerald R. Ford, Vice-President

THE BEST EXAMPLE OF MILITARY LOGIC

Any old brass hat can destroy a village in order to save it. Finer minds transcend the Orwellian cliché.

General J. L. DeWitt, in charge of the Western Defense Command during World War II, recommended the imprisonment of 112,000 American citizens of Japanese descent. In his 1942 report to the Secretary of War, the worthy commander argued that each of the 112,000 was a potential saboteur. Why, then, had no acts of sabotage been reported during the three months following Pearl Harbor? The inscrutable Nip does not disclose his hand so easily. "The very fact that no sabotage has taken place to date," concluded General DeWitt, "is a disturbing and confirming indication that such action will be taken."

THE BEST EXAMPLE OF THE PERSISTENCE OF MILITARY LOGIC

In reply to charges by H. R. Haldeman that the Senate Watergate Committee's interest in Republican wrongdoings was motivated by partisan politics, Chairman Ervin read into the record a letter from the Justice Department stating that it had no evidence of illegal Democratic campaign activities.

Haldeman countered: "The fact that these agencies have searched files and found nothing would confirm that there has been no investigation."

THE BEST EXAMPLE OF TRUTH-IN-PACKAGING

In the preface to *Fielding's Selected Favorites: Hotels and Inns, Europe*, author Fielding explains that his " 'no freeloading' policy is inviolate" and that "recommendations never, never carry price tags . . . From a business standpoint, however, we're faced with a dilemma. Considering today's heavy production costs, no publisher could possibly produce such a specialized book at this price [$3.95, paper] and leave leeway for more than token royalties. Thus, since charity has its limits with any good-willed but indigent author, some of the key hostelries we chose and we decided should be spotlighted have put a small sum against their advertising budgets so that we can tell their stories in greater detail than could normally be considered—a sum, we might add, which merely begins to cover our staggering outlay . . ."

THE BEST EXIT LINE

On April 30, 1956, former Vice-President Alben Barkley, speaking at the commencement exercises of the University of Kentucky, declared, "I would rather sit at the feet of the Lord than dwell in the house of the mighty." He thereupon keeled over and died.

THE BEST EXPLANATION FOR THE STATE OF THE AMERICAN ECONOMY

Bloomingdale's department store sells a sterling silver pendant and chain, personalized with the purchaser's name and Bloomingdale's credit card number. $50.

Should one ever feel the need to venture to some remote

corner of the republic where Bloomie's eight digits do not convey the appropriate status, the traveler might prefer the store's tiny gold ingot on a chain, subtly stamped GOLD. $115.

THE BEST EXPLANATION FOR THE STATE OF THE BRITISH ECONOMY

Every single listing in the London telephone book begins with 01, a handy memory aid for those who might forget the prefix the first few hundred times they dialed. In deference to official optimism on the improved state of British education, the General Post Office (which is in charge of the telephones) has elected to omit similar repetition of other vital instructions—the need to lift the receiver from its cradle, the virtue of waiting for dial tones, etc. Another

47

initiative to modernize service—the plan to save paper by breaking up the London directory into some twenty separate neighborhood volumes—has been tabled. There were some complaints from citizens who would prefer not to sift through twenty alphabetical listings for a single number, we understand.

THE BEST EXPLANATION FOR THE STATE OF THE INDIAN ECONOMY

The kos, a unit of distance in India, may vary from one to three miles in length.

THE BEST FIGHTER AIRCRAFT

In the arms race, money talks. The last-generation supersonic fighters cost about $4 million each, and five nations—the United States, USSR, France, Britain, and Sweden—put up the scratch for independently designed aircraft. But technology marches on. The next generation of airframes, engines, control systems, and weapons to match will cost much, much more; only the United States and the Soviet Union seem to be in a hurry.

For comparison, ponder the mid-sixties models, the planes that dominate the skies over the Sinai and North Vietnam, the F4 Phantoms, French Mirage 3's, and MiG-21's. They are roughly equivalent, though the Israelis, who have intimate knowledge of each, claim to prefer the Phantoms. All have maximum speeds around 1,500 mph, operational ceilings around 50,000 feet, and use heat-seeking missiles or old-fashioned rockets and cannon that require pilot assistance.

The new Russian entry, the Foxbat (NATO names them, not the Russians), can top 2,000 mph at 80,000 feet. What else they can do is a secret. Foxbats are used by the Egyptian Air Force for recon over Israel because neither Phantoms nor ground-to-air missiles can touch them. Only American know-how—a Raytheon air-to-air missile for intercepting the Foxbat is on the way—and Soviet reluctance to escalate in the Middle East will keep the Phantoms from teenage obsolescence.

Not a nation to put its eggs in one defense contractor, America's answer to the Foxbat is four different planes: the Grumman F14 Tomcat, the General Dynamics F111, the McDonnell Douglas F15 Eagle, and the Lockheed YF12. F111's have been around awhile and had a go at combat in Vietnam, but the less said the better about Robert McNamara's adventure in cost-benefit analysis. The Tomcat and Eagle fly only as prototypes, and both will be incredibly expensive replacements for the Phantom. It is, in fact, still unsettled that Congress will shell out to have both built in quantity. The carrier-based Tomcat costs Grumman $25 million each, though they could be forced to make at least token deliveries at the pre-cost-overrun contract price of $16 million. The air force's Eagle is a bargain at only $12 million, and congressional spoilsports want to see it modified to replace the Tomcat as guardian of the nuclear fleet.

In any event, they will be the best fighters below 70,000 feet for quite a while. A Tomcat (probably the classier of the two; the air force ought to remember Cheap-is-Cheap) can maneuver like an old Korean War dogfighter, yet packs an unbelievable arsenal. Its computer can track up to four targets at a time at ranges of nearly 150 miles, then launch Phoenix missiles ($400,000 a throw) to stop them. Should the need arise, a Tomcat can accelerate to about 2,000 mph.

Above 80,000 feet the Foxbat has the edge. But should you doubt the moral fiber of American engineering, the Defense Department will tell you about a potential Lockheed entry. Only a recon version, the SR-71 (nicknamed Blackbird) exists now. But Lockheed's Skunk Works lab would be glad to dust off plans for an eighty-ton fighter variant that could fly at 120,000 feet at 2,500 mph. Don't ask how much it would cost; all-titanium-steel airframes don't come at garage-sale prices, and Lockheed never reckoned with Senator Proxmire when it designed the Blackbird in the mid-sixties. Maybe they can sell it to the Shah of Iran . . .

THE BEST FLAVOR OF BASKIN-ROBBINS ICE CREAM

Of the celebrated 100-plus Baskin-Robbins flavors (31 at a time), few of the most imaginative—Here Comes the Fudge, Bubble Gum, Chocolate Cheesecake, Red, White and Blueberry, Fluffernut—are meant for adults. A purist might opt for either Chocolate Fudge or French Vanilla, the extra-cost, 15-percent-butterfat varieties; to find better, one must make one's own. But for us no flavor surpasses Mandarin Chocolate, the jet-black chocolate sherbet laced with mandarin orange and inspired by the most decadent of true northern Italian ices.

THE BEST FRENCH COOKBOOK

For decades, Anglophobic cooks who wished to go beyond the women's mags' 400 Ways to Mold Lime Jell-O ("chill for 45 minutes before stirring in the drained crab meat and Ritz crackers") had only the supremely able, if bland, *Joy of Cooking* to advise them. Today the neophyte can rely on the first volume of Beck, Bertholle, and Child's *Mastering the Art of French Cooking*, or Lillian Langseth-Christensen's *Basic Recipe Book for Epicures*. Mmes Child et Cie., for example, explain everything: beating egg whites fluffy to puréeing chicken livers. European food terminology—cuts of meat, utensils—are carefully translated to North American equivalents. And where the infinitely patient text might fail, clear line drawings rescue the amateur.

But if you already know that mayonnaise requires egg yolks, oil, a wire whisk, and strong wrists, the standard is Henri-Paul Pellaprat's *Great Book of French Cuisine*. Pellaprat began his career in 1881 at the age of twelve as a pastry chef. He worked his way up to the great French restaurant kitchens, then reigned at the Cordon Bleu Cooking School in Paris until 1932. His 1935 compilation of

2,030 recipes (so the current jacket copy claims; we didn't count) covers the field—from baked pigs' feet with truffle sauce (p. 635) to croquembouche crowned with spun sugar ribbons (p. 1018). Few of them are as easy as they read, but the 300 awesome photographs at least prove that somebody can do it.

THE BEST FRENCH RESTAURANT

Restaurant rating is such an organized activity in France that schools of thought may be discerned. At one pole are the slaves to tradition, partisans who have no difficulty distinguishing the definition of *haute cuisine* from that of great cooking. Their gods are Escoffier, Carême, and perhaps Pellaprat; their favorite restaurants, those with roots in nineteenth-century bourgeois notions of aristocratic pretense. At the other extreme are the Young Turks, food critics who rejoice in simplicity and ultra-fresh ingredients. It is they who have chosen to celebrate Paul Bocuse's Grand Stuff, meals dominated by massive portions of grilled lamb and buttered lima beans. At the moment, the simplicity school is in fashion—today's chefs are more prized for their insight in choosing fresh sea bass than for their ability to sauce the fish afterward.

Curiously enough, the restaurant that symbolized the rise of the New Way has unjustly suffered from the fame of its progeny. Fernand Point's Restaurant de la Pyramide in Vienne revolutionized French cuisine. Point rejected the Sun King's vision of luxury cooking in favor of a cuisine of restraint that emphasized the natural flavors of the raw materials. The result was not a slide down the slippery slope to steak and potatoes, but an enormously disciplined approach to the art. Recipes were tested at staff meals, often for years, before the dishes were included in la Pyramide's repertoire. By Point's death in 1955 one could more appropriately speak of his dominance of rather than his influence on French cooking. No less than five of the sixteen Michelin three-star restaurants are run by ex-Pyramide trainees.

The food hierarchy has never adjusted to the idea of la Pyramide without the master. True, his widow maintained the restaurant with three stars intact, but it was written off as a museum. The critics looked elsewhere for inspiration— to the Alsatian Auberge de l'Ill, to the Troisgros brothers in Roanne, to Bocuse north of Lyons.

Ironically, it is that lack of attention which may explain why la Pyramide is the best restaurant in the world. Bocuse is a bit busy hawking his wine label in American liquor stores. Troisgros and the Haeberlins of the Auberge de l'Ill surely deserve their reputations, but both have lost some of their charm under a barrage of publicity.

La Pyramide is as good as it ever was. The menu has only very recently begun to vary from the old days. Lunch or dinner in the modest dining room typically begins with fresh foie gras in a slice of brioche, then a tiny mousse of trout in a truffled sauce. The fish course might be the famous *gratin de queues d'écrevisses*, or salmon in a white-wine sauce accented by the tartness of tomato. Next, perhaps a roasted duck with flesh still pink, or chicken from Bresse in a cream sauce edged with vinegar. After the cheese course comes an avalanche of desserts—raspberries with raspberry sauce; the ludicrously rich butter cream, chocolate, and hazelnut *marjolaine* cake; a peasant-like sticky pastry tasting faintly of orange; exquisite petits fours. The sherbet offered between rounds may be the most perfect of all Pyramide creations—it simply explodes sour lemon but leaves the mouth unpuckered.

Of course, that description is not overwhelming evidence of superiority. Tales of salmon soufflé at the Auberge de l'Ill or the gâteau of wild strawberries at Le Père Bise are equally impressive. What really sets apart la Pyramide is an intangible quality, a determination to create a refuge from the aggressive pace. It is not that the reception or service at Paul Bocuse is hurried or mechanical, but somehow an awareness of the nearby autoroute with its tailgating Citroëns never completely fades. Chez Point, the greeting from Maître Vincent rings truer, the advice from sommelier Louis seems meant only for you, the inexpensive wines (Condrieu, Beaujolais) more carefully selected. La Pyramide is not only a great restaurant, it is one's vision of a great restaurant.

G THE BEST GRAND TOURING SEDAN

GT's used to be sports cars with enough of the performance edge taken off—softer suspension, more weight in the wrong places—to qualify as luxury sedans. After all, the Beautiful People had to have a way to get around Europe before the era of jets. Today the term is obsolete. A half-dozen automobiles offer *haut bourgeois* comfort and breathtaking acceleration and handling.

Some of the new breed are simply expensively refined mass-market sedans. The Mercedes-Benz 450SE, the Jaguar XJ12, and the BMW 3.0 Coupe come to mind. All are leathered and air-conditioned and power-assisted to the limits. Yet all have the engine and handling to be able to cruise at 100 mph on the autobahn or compete with a Porsche 914 on twisty country roads. Even more impressive are the $20,000-plus, limited-production specialty cars with racing-car antecedents, like the Aston-Martin DBS, the Maserati Indy, and the Lamborghini Espada. There are no real tricks to these cars. Just massive engines, spare-no-expense design, and superior quality control. The Espada, for example, has a twelve-cylinder, four-liter engine with six carburetors, which generates 350 horsepower. It has a top speed of 155 mph and, unlike equally powerful Detroit iron, the engineering to match: the Espada's track is almost five feet wide, each wheel is independently suspended, all four brakes are power-assisted disks.

But the most satisfying of the new GT's is the front-wheel-drive Citroën-Maserati SM. The SM might be an experimental car, something sent around to the auto shows by the manufacturers to attract crowds between model changes. It might be, but it isn't—Citroën is producing about six thousand a year and selling them for $13,500. The guts of the SM are the Citroën hydropneumatic suspension and the elegant Maserati V6. Each wheel is independently served by a hydraulic servo system that pushes fluid around to adjust for load differentials and road conditions. The aluminum-block Maserati engine displaces only

3.0 liters, to beat the French tax on big cars, and keep gas consumption near 20 miles per gallon. But thanks to the SM's aerodynamic body shape and light weight, that is enough to propel it at up to 135 mph.

At such speeds an ordinary luxury-car power-steering gear would become useless and even dangerous. Citroën agrees and has built a remarkable alternative. The steering is very quick but enormously stable, because the self-centering mechanism itself is power-assisted. Moreover, as the SM accelerates, the power steering gradually cuts out to compensate for high-speed instability.

Citroën attention extends to the passenger compartment. The leather contour bucket seats adjust in every possible dimension, as does the steering column; the air conditioning and FM stereo (standard equipment) are the best on any car; the controls are well thought out; a master panel signals malfunction in any of thirteen systems.

THE BEST HAMBURGER

The best hamburger is to be found at the Campus Dining Room Restaurant and Bar, 119th Street and Amsterdam Avenue, New York City.

Another provincial New York entry, you say? Yet another insult to the reading public from Gotham chauvinists unaware that America lies on the Newark side of the Hudson?

Not so. The true hamburger is a dying institution, and it's dying faster in the Land of the Real People than in the city. In this age of increasing polarization (well, the age of increasing polarization seems to have ended recently, but the metaphor is too good to waste) the hamburger has not been spared. Honest ground meat on a bun has been transformed into either

(a) 1½ ounces of steamed beef disc in carbohydrate wrapper for 59¢ (nice on its own terms, actually; very regressed), or

(b) 12 ounces of Ye Olde Freshlye Choppede Sir Loin On Oure Owne [bill of sale shown on request] Sesame Seedede Rolle for $2.95.

By contrast, the Campus hamburger owes nothing to Ronald McDonald or Robert Morley. Discipline and dedication, however, lie behind the seemingly effortless activities of the counterman. The three- to four-ounce burger is neither too fat nor too lean, the latter a common error among the affluent. It is neither frozen nor precooked; the grill is a gas-fired iron short-order range, rather than charcoal, wood, or microwave. The bun is toasted crisp on the meat side, yet only warmed on the outside. Mayo (decadent, but acceptable), lettuce, tomato on request.

THE BEST HOPE FOR A CURE FOR CANCER

Cancer can be cured today, if you are very lucky. Relatively few varieties—some leukemias, liver, pancreas, gall bladder—are simple death sentences. The trick is to catch the aberrant cells early, when there are few of them around, and when they are lodged at a single site. In general, the "best" place to get cancer is a spot where it is easily diagnosed and where the affected organ isn't crucial to life: the skin, the lips, the salivary glands. Five-year survival rates for all these cancers is better than 80 percent. That is actually better than it sounds, since most of the victims are old people for whom half a decade is a decent statistical lifetime.

Like most of medicine, cancer treatment is an inexact science. Cancer is about basic life processes, and we know very little about life. Hence the weapons are rather crude: if the malignancy is small and accessible to the knife, excise it (and everything nearby) and hope the monster hasn't wandered into the bloodstream or the lymph ducts. If the cancer has spread, or is inconveniently diffused—Hodgkin's disease, leukemia—plaster it with radiation or chemicals. Both work, because cancer cells in the act of reproduction are more vulnerable than well-behaved normal cells.

None of these procedures, however, has a particularly good track record for cures. For every John Wayne there are ten Edward R. Murrows. Either the treatment fails to get all the malignant cells, or it does so much damage to healthy tissue that the body is destroyed. For the moment, cure largely means delay. As a strategy for saving lives, the most promising approach lies in early detection of the big killing cancers that quietly engulf internal organs before they cause overt symptoms: colon, breast, uterus.

A true cure awaits a conceptual breakthrough—some insight into the cause of cancer or the life-style of the cancer cell that permits an interruption of the growth process. Two directions of attack have attracted researchers. One is to find differences in the life chemistry between normal and malignant cells, and then selectively to deprive the cancerous ones of some environmental factor necessary for survival. Cancer cells may need a different set of enzymes, the intermediaries of so much of the chemistry of life, to set up housekeeping in a healthy organ. Perhaps the key is to neutralize the activity of such enzymes or prevent their production at the site.

An even hotter research approach is predicated on the theory that cancer is a failure of the body's immune system to do its job. Alien living organisms—bacteria, viruses, foreign cells—are ordinarily overwhelmed by a militia of natural sentries. Strikingly, people who have immune-deficiency diseases or have taken drugs to prevent the immunological rejection of organ transplants seem especially vulnerable to cancer as well as to standard microorganisms. The circumstantial evidence of a link between cancer and the immune response is even more compelling: cancer is largely a disease of old people whose immune capacity is demonstrably failing. Some scientists theorize that the production of cancer cells is a common accident, but only in the immunologically weak do they gain a foothold.

The answer may be to stimulate natural defenses against malignancy the way vaccines stimulate natural defenses against virus diseases. Two of the honchos of cancer research—Robert Good of Sloan-Kettering, Edmund Klein at Roswell Park in Buffalo—are fairly committed to the notion. Klein has gotten results with both skin and breast cancer. The disadvantage to date is that the immune response works best on small tumors. But then lots of things work on small tumors . . .

THE BEST HOPE FOR A POLLUTION-FREE ENGINE

Detroit can, and probably reluctantly will, produce in the next ten years an automobile engine that generates almost no air pollution. But the way things are going, that engine is unlikely to solve much of the air pollution problem.

There are two ways to purify engine exhausts: build an engine that burns cleanly, or tack pollution-reducing devices onto dirty engines. Nearly all auto manufacturers are committed to the second approach. There is no question they will succeed—the technology needed is unrevolutionary. The trouble is, these devices need constant maintenance if they are to work once they leave the factory. Most states seem unable to enforce minimum safety maintenance standards. How likely are they to make pollution standards stick? And even if the states should find the backbone for the job, where will the mechanics come from to service the delicate devices?

The alternative is to design a new engine. The rotary engine—the so-called Wankel—has been touted as the clean engine, and in fact the rotary made by Mazda is the first to meet 1975 federal pollution standards. But rotaries are not inherently clean, just small and light. Mazda used the extra room under the hood to install an elaborate pollution control system. Other auto companies and private inventors have invested in attempts to build a steam turbine engine. Large steam turbines are the most efficient practical converters of heat to motion. However, adaptation to the automobile is difficult—the engine must warm up well in advance, and under any condition it will resist rapid acceleration. Steam turbine buses and trucks are on the way, but probably not cars.

Another, less publicized design, the stratified-charge engine, is more promising. The stratified-charge engine offers a solution to the major technical snag in cleaning up internal combustion engines. If you burn gasoline at a low temperature, the incomplete combustion leaves carbon monoxide and hydrocarbon to foul the exhaust. Raise the engine temperature, and the carbon is completely consumed, but nitrogen from the air tends to combine with oxygen near the center of combustion to form a whole new set of dangerous pollutants. The stratified-charge engine beats this bind by burning the fuel twice in one or more chambers. The only drawback: low engine efficiency, a problem that also plagues conventional engines burdened by pollution control systems. To date, only Honda has produced an SC engine for sale in the United States. Ford and Chrysler are supposed to be interested.

THE BEST HORROR MOVIE

A difficult category, because the definition of horror is so vague. Does Hitchcock's *Psycho* count as horror or suspense? What of Tod Browning's *Freaks*, an underground classic that many find the most revolting movie ever made?

We shall stay clear of such cinematographic heights and choose only from the minor peaks of contemporary mass culture. Thus we must also exclude *King Kong* and *Frankenstein*, works so successful they transcend the medium.

One possibility for top honors is *Them*, a 1954 film most notable for its seminal investigation of the effects of atomic radiation from bomb testing on insect life. The climax, a shootout with radiation-mutated giant ants, takes place in the famous storm sewer system of Los Angeles. In the same genre, but less to our taste, is the much-praised *The Fly*. Here the insect motif is preserved, but with an ironic twist: the protagonist is trapped in the body of a housefly—a crude, derivative, but effective metaphor of human frustration and impotence. Real horror purists might prefer *The Night of the Living Dead*. By the standard of the medium, *Night* has never been surpassed. All this tale of the rising of ghouls from the bowels of Pittsburgh lacks is a sense of irony.

Our own candidate for the best, however, is *Invasion of the Body Snatchers* (1956). A small town is taken over by aliens who grow duplicates of each citizen and substitute them for the real people. There is no confrontation with monsters, no pseudoscientific razzle-dazzle. Instead, horror is the well-constructed, internally consistent fantasy of a paranoid schizophrenic.

THE BEST HOUSEPLANT FOR A DARK APARTMENT

All houseplants need some light. But a good number make do with small amounts of indirect sun and positively flourish in a patch of northern-exposure window light. This is not because of some miraculous new advance in horticulture. Most of these plants are simply native to tropical rain forests and have evolved in the nearly perpetual shade of dominant foliage.

Probably the commonest are the philodendrons. The majority are fast-growing climbers that need humid warmth, a fair amount of water, and good drainage— though in fact they have been known to tolerate much less. The pleasing, if familiar, *Monstera deliciosa* (Swiss cheese plant) is one member of the family that is a bit fussy.

63

A really tough, equally clichéd subdued-light plant is the Chinese evergreen, distinctive for its dark-green leaves accented with white. Still another, and one of the handsomest in the category, is the dwarf palm (*Chamaedorea elegans*). Its long bamboolike canes mysteriously transform themselves into delicate, densely leaved stalks. The palm is not, however, up to much neglect; it is troubled by dust on the leaves, a variety of standard insects, and low humidity. Others capable of making do without direct sun include the corn plant, the arrowhead, and the snow pine.

Flowering plants in the family are rare. Two exceptions, the *Spathiphyllum* and the *Clivia*, may bloom in poor light. Both produce trumpet-shaped flowers; the *Clivia*'s are even snowy-white.

THE BEST HOUSEPLANT TO FORGET ABOUT ON VACATION

One big family of houseplants—succulents—can be left for weeks without attention. They easily adapt to arid conditions, since they are almost all desert plants; probably the greatest problem in raising them is resisting the urge to drench their parched stalks.

Most plants depend on the soil for moisture from day to day. Since the leaf structure of the average houseplant has evolved to provide the maximum possible exposure to light, the leaves quickly lose what water they hold through evaporation. Succulents manage by storing surplus water, by minimizing surface evaporation, and by reacting to really extreme drought by becoming dormant.

The cacti (technically, members of the family Cactaceae) available in plant stores are the most common of succulents. But their alien appearance and usual thorns hardly qualify them to warm up a bleak room. Succulents, however, do come in less-threatening, houseplant-like shapes. Sedums are tough little plants with masses of tiny fat leaves that grow all the way down to the base of the stalk. Given half a chance, a broken stem will take root and start a new colony. Kalanchoes, other hardy, rapid-growing succulents, come in a dozen leaf shades from soft purple to soft yellow. They are warm-weather plants that can be tricked into flowering indoors in the winter. Aloes look more like desert vegetation, with their great sheaths of speckled, century-plant-like leaves and lonely central stalks. Given some time, they will fill a great pot with more aloes via underground runners from the parent.

I THE BEST ILLUSTRATION OF THE "CONVERGENCE THEORY" THAT COMMUNIST AND CAPITALIST SOCIETIES WILL COME INCREASINGLY TO RESEMBLE ONE ANOTHER

The late French President Georges Pompidou and Russian Communist Party Chairman Leonid Brezhnev shared a common hobby: collecting expensive cars. Brezhnev has two Rolls-Royces and a Cadillac thoughtfully given to him by President Nixon on his 1972 trip to the Soviet Union.

THE BEST ILLUSTRATOR

Thomas Bewick (1753–1828).

THE BEST INSTANT COFFEE

One might argue the relative merits of freeze-dried versus regular; Chase & Sanborn even has a brand that combines the two. But there really isn't much point. No instant coffee tastes like coffee, and all the standard brands share the piquant flavor of freshly brewed Cuyahoga River water. Not unreasonably, the major conclusion of a consumer survey of forty-five instants was: the weaker the brew, the better the cup . . .

For those in need of a caffeine hype who have somehow misplaced their Melitta's and No-Doz bottles, we would reluctantly recommend Kava. Kava no more resembles coffee than Dom Pérignon. However, the natural acid in the coffee beans is chemically neutralized, making it possible to drink Kava strong without contracting terminal shudder.

T THE BEST JET (PRIVATE) UNDER $1,000,000

If money is no object, the Boeing Corporation will be happy to sell you a 727 equipped to fly twenty across the Atlantic in consummate luxury. Hugh Hefner preferred the trimmer DC-9—not quite the range or elbow room of the Boeing Tri-jet, but ever so much more economical, what with the cost of hi-test gasoline these days. McDonnell Douglas even has some "pre-owned" DC-9's on sale under $3 million.

For those who must really count pennies, there is still the Cessna Citation, a six-passenger jet for $725,000 (base price, stripped). Cessna has had great success with the little Citation, advertising it as a prestigious step up from similar-size propeller-driven craft—a plane to sell in, or be seen in, at Bar Harbor. That may all be true, but the budget price is reflected in the budget speed—only 400 mph—and budget fuel capacity—it has a range of just 1,300 miles. At the same price, the Italian Rinaldo Piaggio Corporation markets a stripped-down business version of a light jet, the PD-808, which it developed with government funds. The PD-808 does not skimp on power; its twin engines allow a cruising speed above 500 mph. The plane is, however, a fuel hog (the range is only 1,400 miles) and a runway hog —it needs 6,300 feet for landing, more than a DC-9 or 727.

To beat these drawbacks you pay a price—expect an extra $400,000. For a shade over $1 million, there's the West German Hansa, the French Falcon 10 (vended in America by Pan Am), and Rockwell International's Sabreliner. Israeli Aircraft Industries' 1123 Westwind is typical of the group: a range of 2,100 miles, cruising speed 500 mph, a healthy 4,000-feet-a-minute climb rate, a modest 3,100-foot landing requirement.

One plane, however, defies the arithmetic—the Gates Learjet. More Learjets have been sold than any other business jet, and for good reason. This jet does everything its beefier cousins can. Carries six and a crew of two, cruises above 500 mph, climbs like a fighter (6,800 feet/minute), and goes 2,000 miles between fill-ups. Yet you can get delivery at the Wichita, Kansas, factory for less than $900,000. The secret is exceptional efficiency. An empty Learjet weighs 6,800 pounds and can load on 6,600 pounds of people, fuel, and baggage. By comparison, a Westwind weighs 13,500 pounds and carries only 7,000 more.

That efficiency did not come from some fancy computer simulation, or teams of aeronautical engineers slaving for months over a hot wind tunnel. The Learjet's inventor, William Lear, is the last of the successful backyard entrepreneurs. An airplane's wings usually cost a minimum of a million dollars to design. He managed it by himself in consultation with a talented neighborhood auto body repair man.

Lear, incidentally, sold his plane to the Gates Tire and Rubber Corporation in 1966 for a bundle and retired to the desert to invent a pollution-free auto engine. Lightning, alas, does not strike thrice (Lear also invented the eight-track car stereo); the best he has come up with to date is a steam engine for buses, of uncertain merit.

L THE BEST LIVING THEORETICAL PHYSICIST

No contest, if you take the word of the Nobel Committee. John Bardeen of the University of Illinois has won the physics prize twice. As part of a Bell

Labs group in the late forties he researched the eccentric behavior of electric current in crystalline materials known as semiconductors. The result: transistors, and a key to solid-state electronics miniaturization. Bardeen has since broken new ground in an entirely different field. He helped develop an explanation of why electrical resistance in some metals and compounds disappears when they are chilled to within a few degrees of absolute zero. Just as important, he showed it was possible to produce the same magic at less extreme (hence less expensive) temperatures. This super-conductivity phenomenon is now exploited in constructing incredibly sensitive laboratory instruments and may eventually revolutionize computer design.

We think, however, the honor belongs in particle physics, not because practitioners in other fields are less worthy, but because they are asking less important questions. Particle physicists test the frontiers in an attempt to explain the fundamental nature of matter. Perhaps the grandest mystery of physics is what happens within atoms, to explain reactions so rapid between particles so small that ordinary brands of intuition are useless.

Consider the least-understood part of the problem, the interaction of particles inside atomic nuclei. Here particles act on each other at distances of about 0.000000000000001 inches, and unstable particles can be created and destroyed within 0.000000000000000000000001 seconds. Reams of data have been collected by accelerating tiny fragments of matter to close to the speed of light, smashing them into targets, and then capturing photographic records of the resulting debris. The most distinguished of the theoreticians trying to find order in this high-energy chaos is Murray

Gell-Mann at Cal Tech. The name of the game is to explain the existence of the fifty-odd particles identified in the general framework of modern physics. Gell-Mann, who in one way or another is associated with virtually every aspect of particle theory, discovered powerful predictive symmetries between particles, relationships he immodestly christened the "Eightfold Way."

THE BEST LOGICAL PUZZLE

It has been dubbed Newcomb's Paradox, after its originator, William Newcomb, a physicist at the University of California. But for the historically minded, the John Calvin Memorial Puzzle would be a more appropriate name.

A rich Martian comes to town and offers a game with anyone who wishes to play. He (or she, the sex of Martians is never obvious) produces two boxes. Box One is made of glass and contains a thousand-dollar bill; Box Two is opaque, but the Martian announces that either it is empty, or it contains one million dollars. You may choose to take the contents of both boxes (a possible $1,001,000) or only those of Box Two (a possible $1,000,000).

The Martian, however, is a superb judge of the human personality and does not like to give away more than a million dollars in a single game. Thus, if he thinks you will take both boxes, Box Two will be empty and your total take will be just $1,000. If he thinks you will take only Box Two, that box will contain the million. The Martian further cautions that he has played the game at least one hundred times in a neighboring town and he has never guessed wrong. Every person who has opted for Box Two, alone, has found a million; every person who has taken both has ended up with $1,000. Martians, by the way, are constitutionally incapable of lying.

What should you do? The answer seems obvious—take both boxes. Once the Martian offers to play with you, the die is cast. He cannot change the contents of Box Two, so you have nothing to lose by accepting both.

Or is it so obvious? Dozens of people before have followed that logic, and all of them lost the million. By contrast, no one who has been sufficiently impressed by the Martian's previous record to bypass the sure thousand has not been sorry afterward. You *know* it can't hurt to take both boxes, but then, so did all those losers. Put it another way—the Martian is willing to entertain side bets from observers. Who in his right mind would bet against the Martian after watching his unbroken string of successful guesses?

THE BEST LONDON RESTAURANT

The trouble with eating in London is that it is like eating in New York. There are vast hordes longing to dine well and dozens of exciting new restaurants longing to fill the void. Yet somehow nothing seems quite to work out. Perhaps it is only a scarcity of talent—running a restaurant well demands more than one chef imported from the Continent. More likely it's incentives. There aren't enough people who both know good food and are willing to pay for it. Restaurants are made or broken by who shows up, not by what is served. The few establishments that start out with standards find little reason to maintain them. No guidebook inspector will turn the decline into headlines; no army of food pedants will organize a boycott.

Of course, there are a few bright spots. Robert Carrier's relentless pursuit of the *nouveau* may irritate the snob, but the fixed menus frequently work well. Inigo Jones's lovely room can make up for an occasional error in service. The fish is very fresh (and very expensive) at Wilton's. The new Capital Hotel dining room produces the best rack of lamb north of Paris. Marynka demonstrates that Polish food is no joke.

But for our money we'll take London's Indian/Pakistani restaurants. They tend to be much more sophisticated than the North American version and not nearly so lacking in grace. The best of them, Sri Lanka, is in fact not Indian but Ceylonese, a variant on the national cuisines of the subcontinent. This pretty little restaurant near Earls Court (an unsocial twenty-minute taxi ride west from Mayfair) prepares the predictable curries, flavored rices, and breads as well as any other in London and adds a dozen distinguished Ceylonese specialties. Among them, a super-hot tomato broth (perhaps really a purée of chili peppers), the pleasure of which comes in the vibration of subtler spices in the aftertaste; delicate rice-flour crêpes served with fried eggs; chewy fried breads stuffed with egg, vegetables, or meat, and far superior to the usual Indian paratha; a steamed rice-flour cake drowned in coconut milk. With a couple of German lagers, the bill comes to about five dollars per person.

M THE BEST MEAL IN ISRAEL

Fresh fruit. The plums are especially good.

THE BEST MOVIE CRITIC

John Simon is the movie critic of record, the critic whose reviews are least likely to sound silly in fifty years. Nice people are puzzled by his ferocity, but the only puzzling thing is how he can sit through two hundred movies a year unaided by Dexedrine, yet remain above misanthropy.

In circles where name-dropping is of the essence, he is known as Simon the Bad, mainly for his flogging of the helpless:

On *Getting Straight:*

Candice Bergen's pseudoacting continues not to improve. By some dire misconception, if a pretty girl makes faces, screams, and assumes agonized attitudes, the result passes for a performance. Even that whining voice of Miss Bergen's makes one wish Papa's ventriloquizing would come to her aid. The film contains the obligatory nudity, though not for Miss Bergen, whose insufficiencies force the prying camera into truly Pascalian leaps—from shoulders to toes, usually.

On *The Strawberry Statement:*

We are always encouraged to envision the orgy just around the next turn of the reel, but all we get is puppy-love, puppy-politics, and Stuart Hagmann's, the director's, insufferable manipulations. His maniacal use of the zoom lens makes that instrument second in hatefulness only to a dentist's drill. Actually it is as if Hagmann were giving the camera incessant hotfoots, making the poor thing leap like a demented creature and land in the unlikeliest places. When it is not zooming, the camera seems to be passed back and forth between a spastic dromomaniac and a whirling dervish. The film makes you seasick.

But Simon reserves his real fury for the super con artists in the ultimate con man's art form:

At the meeting of the film-maker Jacques Demy and the musician Michel Legrand, the best we might have hoped for is Claudelian silence . . . For I doubt that two poorer specimens ever found each other, to produce, not dignified silence, but a ludicrous movie musical. *The Umbrellas of Cherbourg,* which won the 1964 grand prize at Cannes, is distinguished by the fact that its every utterance—from *bonjour* to "fill up the tank with super"—is subjected to a sonorous deviation alleged to be music and singing . . . We are told that in Paris the opening-night audience wept and the critics were ecstatic. It would have made a little more sense the other way round.

Has the emperor no clothes? How marvelous! Who wants clothes anyway? There is more enterprise in walking naked. Nudity is so much more daring and more real. Well, that may be so in the case of avowed nudity, in nudity for a purpose, say, to show off a glorious body. But Godard's films pretend to clothes . . . In fact, however, they are nothing: not even nudity, only skeletons, and even those artificial, made of cardboard.

Simon the Hunter, tracking his prey, may be more fun to read. But lest one forget, Simon the Critic also celebrates the great:

The most poetic and profound film of recent times is Hiroshi Teshigahara's *Woman in the Dunes* . . . Everything in the film is a little stylized and fantasmagoric: the dialogue takes on a dreamlike antilogic which is nonetheless ineluctable, the editing is slightly elliptical to convey a disquieting sense of unexpected intensities in the midst of the quotidian, the unobstrusively brilliant photography is infinitely suggestive in its extreme close-ups in which every grain of sand and every pore of human flesh is obsessively scrutinized until the ripples of flesh and flutters of sand merge in an orgiastic marriage of man and nature.

THE BEST MUSEUM TO TAKE A KID TO IN NEW YORK

The obvious answer is the American Museum of Natural History. This great Romanesque/classical/modern stone pile has everything: one of the world's most spectacular collections of dinosaurs; fantastic animal mock-ups including a ninety-foot blue whale fashioned from fiberglass; a recreation of an African velt; fine plastic models showing all too realistically the development of the human fetus. The trouble is, it seems to be everybody else's obvious answer. You must compete for viewing space with the three or four million kids who are bused in annually.

If you would prefer a more modest but less popular museum, a fine choice would be the Fire Department Museum near City Hall. The best part is the collection of antique firefighting equipment, including an 1820 pumper with a leather hose, and an early steam-powered pumper. The lesser memorabilia and overtly educational exhibits are only so-so.

But our sentimental favorite was (alas, it's closed) the Chase Manhattan Bank Money Museum. The Money

Museum was irresistible to any middle-class kid, at least until he had been introduced to the works of Paul Goodman. One gallery was devoted to foreign currencies and a little anthropology intended to add redeeming social significance. The other had a vast collection of U.S. coins and bills. Among the exotica: a $100,000 bill, a pile of checks endorsed by American Presidents, a check "written" on steel armor plate that was canceled by machine-gun bullets.

THE BEST NATIONAL PARK

It's true you may contract lung cancer from the auto exhausts at Yosemite, or get trampled in the crowd around Yellowstone's Old Faithful. But most of the parks, most of the time, are incredible. The Everglades are a million-and-a-half-acre swamp hugging the tip of Florida, a tangle of tidal pools, grassy shallows, and mangrove rivers, which houses all manner of tropical animals and plants. Hawaii Volcanoes National Park allows the possibility of seeing lava flows, or hiking the lava fields to Mauna Loa's 13,000-foot summit. The Virgin Islands Park on St. John has fine snorkeling on its reef and includes an underwater trail safe enough for beginners. Even Yosemite can be fun at the peak of the season—98 percent of the park is backpacking country in the High Sierras.

The best, however, is still the least accessible: Mount Mc-Kinley National Park in Alaska. Just 250 miles from the Arctic Circle and partially covered by glacial remnants of the Ice Age, the huge park provides limitless vistas of alpine tundra and great mountain peaks. Herds of caribou numbering in the thousands graze the valleys in the summer, while a variety of bighorn sheep can be seen with binoculars on the mountain slopes, some two thousand feet above the timberline. Mount McKinley itself towers 17,000 feet above its base and permanent snows blanket the last two vertical miles.

THE BEST NEW YORK CLUB

More a matter of definitions than personal taste. If the best is the hardest to join, the Knickerbocker or Union is first. The membership runs to the Mayflower Crowd and those who managed to make their money before the income tax and the Securities and Exchange Commission. The richest clubs are the Brook and Links. Money gets you further than social standing, but both can be helpful. The Links could boast (it would be out of character) of six Rockefellers and a Du Pont; the Brook of Marshall Field (department stores), Walter Hoving (jewelry), and John Kennedy (real estate).

Of course, if you expect more than a good martini-and-broiled-salmon lunch, or a deep leather chair and the latest copy of *Barron's*, other clubs can be attractive. The Racquet and Tennis Club has the best athletic facilities in the city: the usual squash courts and swimming pool, the unusual racquet courts, and the almost unique court tennis courts. The latter is an eighteenth-century game favored by the house of Bourbon, whose traditions are being carried on practically singlehandedly by George Plimpton.

If good talk is your game, there is a lot of it at the Century Club. Here achievement means more than caste or money. William Buckley and Arthur Schlesinger, Jr., are members, as are John Lindsay, Philip Johnson, and the upper editorial echelons of *The New York Times*. No achievement, however, will gain admission (unescorted) for Susan Sontag, Mary McCarthy, or Golda Meir; the Century is for men only.

One club that discriminates against men and women equally—and our choice for the best—is the River Club. Apart from the obvious virtues of coeducation, the River has indoor tennis, a swimming pool, squash courts, and passable food. It also has little of the stuffy Old New York formality of a midtown club, and even less of the feeling that paperback rights, office buildings, and judgeships are being sold between courses at lunch.

THE BEST NEW YORK RESTAURANT

French food doesn't seem to travel well when it is exported to the United States. Something about the cost of labor and lack of patrons who will swear allegiance at fifty dollars a head, we think. One might argue that the best national cuisine in New York is Chinese. That is surely true, but no single restaurant manages to prepare it consistently. Eggplant with garlic sauce and similar perfections require skill to prepare, and the skill rarely stays in one establishment for long.

The Coach House, a small, elegant restaurant occupying an old carriage house in the Village, manages both quality and consistency. Addicts are likely to feel the beginning of a food buzz almost as soon as they enter—patrons must pass a dessert display on their way to the dining rooms, the kind of display every food head remembers from the first visit to France. Take a banquette on the ground floor, and the atmosphere is upper middle class New York expensive restaurant: plush and comfortable, but no privacy to be had. Upstairs the decoration is well-bred New England, the tables nicely spread out.

The menu defies easy ethnic classification. You could call it Continental if the AAA motoring guides hadn't finished off that word for good. Most of the more complicated dishes are a variation on the French—steamed striped bass in a garlicky broth, rack of lamb with a delicate glaze, a lovely cold eggplant Provençale appetizer. But a good portion of the food is American. Proper prime ribs, black bean soup, perfect pecan pie. To add to the confusion, the lobster tails are cooked with Mediterranean herbs and feta cheese.

The wine list is at best B+. All the regions are covered, but nothing catches the eye in particular, and the Bordeaux offered are almost all too young. Constantly changing *petits châteaux* listings, however, show some real style and are modestly priced.

If you manage to pace yourself through the complete dinner—harder than it looks, thanks to the miraculous appearance of hot corn sticks with the first course and salad untouched by the dread iceberg—you will be rewarded with the best desserts within four hours' flight. A cake that resembles a mousse supersaturated with chocolate; the *daquoise*, a mocha pastry not unlike textured butter. All this costs about as much as lunch at the Côte Basque—it is hard to spend more than thirty dollars per person unless you insist on drinking Château Ausone with the lamb.

THE BEST NEW YORKER *NEWSBREAK*

You know, the squibs at the bottom of the page to fill up blank space. *The New Yorker* has managed to turn filler into an art form. Some people read them immediately after the cartoons and Antartex ads; others view them as dessert at the end of particularly heavy articles on ecology and the like.

For the student (connoisseur) of the newsbreak, the lowest form is the typographical error that turns an ordinary news item into nonsense:

> Pat Goodnight, Taos, won $50 for first place in the hoop dancing competition. Miss Freddy Stevens, a Navajo, was second. and an inlaid belt buckle third.
> —*Gallup (New Mexico) Daily Independent*

A giant step above such frivolities are typos that make sense in context, those happy coincidences, or linotype operators' Freudian slips:

> For Sale: Baby furniture—all in goo condition
> —*Westport Town Crier*

Of equally high quality—and a true *New Yorker* specialty —are examples of butchered prose, or wildly mixed metaphors that destroy some perfectly mundane exposition:

> Japanese surgeons have succeeded in putting together the opened flesh and skin with a binding fluid in two minutes after an appendectomy, dispensing with the usual sewing.
> Tokyo University Hospital surgeons had been testing the "instant surgery" on dogs and rabbits since February last year and after 70 cases tried it on two human patients.
> The first patient left the hospital two days after his operation. He was alive.
> —*Manila Chronicle*

But surely the purest and best notion of the art is the kind that a steady hand on the keyboard or freshman English lessons on syntax could not prevent. From the thousands, we offer two; take your pick:

> The ten minute walk described corresponds to the class break time. If the class break were extended in length the students would be able to walk farther between classes.
> —*Princeton Alumni Weekly*

Of course, as Ophelia remarked in "Hamlet": "There's rosemary for remembrance . . ."

If she were talking today, she might have added: "and it

also gives a terrific boost to lamb dishes and soups and stews and you wouldn't believe what it does for beef if you sprinkle it on before roasting."

—American Weekly

THE BEST NIXON LINE

"Sure there are dishonest men in local government. But there are dishonest men in national government too."

—Richard M. Nixon, President

THE BEST NONPRESCRIPTION
PAIN-KILLING DRUG

Nothing is better than aspirin, and no widely marketed brand of aspirin is better than any other. Aspirin has been around a long time—about seventy-five years. No one understands why it relieves pain or reduces fever and arthritic inflammation, but it does work, and its side effects have been carefully catalogued. The German pharmaceutical house of Bayer once held the American patent on aspirin and has managed to dominate the market ever since. There is, however, not the slightest validity to Bayer's claims to pain-relieving superiority over brands that sell for one third the price.

Such are the ways of American commerce that there is little effective control on the marketing of analgesics that are equivalent or inferior to aspirin. Many are combinations of aspirin and less well known painkillers. The most common "extra added ingredients" are phenacetin and salicylamide. Neither is in any way superior to the real thing. Phenacetin has even been suspected of exacerbating kidney ailments. Some manufacturers toss in a little caffeine or antihistamine. The former, in the dosage included in the pill, has no effect on pain; the latter is a mild sedative.

One of the side effects of aspirin is irritation to the stomach lining. Hence the inclusion of some antacid in Bufferin and its imitators. The trouble is, antacid can't really do the job. A preferred alternative is to use acetaminophen (its most popular brand name is Tylenol), which is about as effective as aspirin and does not cause gastric irritation. Acetaminophen does not, however, reduce arthritic inflammation. Those who must use aspirin can cut the irritation by using a soluble form like Alka-Seltzer.

THE BEST NON SEQUITUR

Ku Klux Klan poster:

> THE ONLY REASON YOU ARE WHITE
> TODAY IS BECAUSE YOUR ANCESTORS
> BELIEVED AND PRACTICED SEGREGATION

THE BEST PAIN-KILLING DRUG

The most potent of all analgesics is the derivative of opium known as heroin. Ironically, heroin was first introduced as a substitute for another pain-killing opium derivative, morphine, on the premise that it would not cause addiction. It is not legally available for the treatment of patients in the United States for any purpose, and the street price can run as high as $100,000 a pound. Luckily, other less effective chemical derivatives of opium are legal, and they comprise the only remotely satisfactory weapons in the treatment of severe pain.

The drawbacks of opium derivatives are obvious. All create physical and psychological dependence, all require increasing dosages to sustain pain relief, all cause some degree of drowsiness and respiratory depression. Which is best depends upon which side effects are least obnoxious to

85

the patient. For intense pain after surgery, physical and emotional dependence are unimportant—the need for the analgesic will rapidly disappear. Morphine and Dilaudid, both of which are exceedingly addictive, are often used. But for the chronically ill, the trade-offs between side effects and analgesia can become very important. Demerol produces only mild withdrawal symptoms, but generates enough of a high to create substantial emotional dependence. Methadone, still another opium derivative, produces almost no withdrawal symptoms at all (hence its standard use), but seems to be as psychologically addictive as morphine. Percodan, a combination of opiates and other drugs, is only moderately addictive, but is much less effective than morphine or Dilaudid.

The primary alternative to morphine-related drugs is codeine. Codeine scores well in terms of addictive properties, but is far less potent an analgesic. One experiment has even suggested that it is no more effective than aspirin when used in modest dosage. Darvon, a distant chemical relative of methadone, is also attractive as a less addictive painkiller. Its analgesic properties, however, are not as well documented as those of codeine.

THE BEST PASSAGE FROM THE UNITED STATES TAX CODE

The righteously indignant particularly enjoy the following passage, one from tax expert Philip Stern's collection: "For the purposes of Paragraph (3), an organization described in Paragraph (2) shall be deemed to include an organization described in Section 501 (c)(3)." Good, though hardly great. No contract worth the two-point type it was printed in would be caught dead without something akin.

A connoisseur will recognize that creativity is best expressed in private tax bills, those amendments to the code intended to help a certain special someone. Stockholders of the Twin Cities Rapid Transit Company have a more than sentimental attachment to one of former Senator Eugene McCarthy's less lyrical compositions, his bill "Income Tax Treatment of Certain Losses Sustained in Converting Street Railway to Bus Operations." But the critical mind must note its ultimate failure within the context of the literature of tax—the author too obviously rejects the medium as a legitimate form of self-expression.

How can it be compared with Senator Russell Long's exuberant, yet disciplined celebration of the art in his private bill for New Orleans TV Station WWL. The first three clauses of the amendment read:

(a) Which consists of . . .
(b) Which is carried on by . . .
(c) Less than ten per cent of the net income of which . . .

THE BEST PATRIOTIC
PREP-SCHOOL POEM

THE SIEGE OF BELGRADE

An Austrian army, awfully arrayed,
Boldly by battery besieged Belgrade;
Cossack commanders cannonading come,
Dealing destruction's devastating doom.
Ev'ry endeavour engineers essay,
For fame, for fortune fighting—furious fray!
Generals 'gainst generals grapple—gracious Good,
How honours Heaven heroic hardihood!
Infuriate, indiscriminate in ill,
Kindred kill kinsmen—kinsmen kindred kill!
Labour low levels loftiest, longest lines;
Men march 'mid mounds, 'mid moles, 'mid murderous mines.
Now noisy, noxious numbers notice nought
Of outward obstacles opposing ought:
Poor patriots, partly purchased, partly pressed,
Quite quaking, quickly quarter quest.
Reason returns, religious right redounds
Suwarrow stops such sanguinary sounds:
Truce to thee, Turkey—triumph to thy train!
Unjust, unwise, unmerciful Ukraine!

Why wish we warfare? Wherefore welcome where
Xerxes, Ximenes, Xanthus, Xavier?
Yield, yield, ye youths! ye yeomen, yield your yell!
Zeno's, Zopater's, Zoroaster's zeal,
Attracting all, arts against arms appeal.

—*The Trifler* (1817)

THE BEST PEANUT BUTTER

Some of life's greatest pleasures are taken for granted or dulled by snobbery. Surely peanut butter, the cheapest and most nutritous of foods, fits the category. For those who do not consider themselves up from PB and J, memories of Art Baker and *You Asked for It* make Skippy the Proustian favorite. But the best is actually a crass newcomer, Jif, the one with the obscene TV ads starring the Mother Who Wants Only the Finest for Her Child. Jif simply smells and tastes more like peanuts. There is no real competition.

THE BEST ORGANIC PEANUT BUTTER

Surely, Deaf Smith's. Many other brands squeeze out the oil and sell it separately, a process that leaves the product more aesthetic but less tasty.

THE BEST PEPPERIDGE FARM COOKIE

Fiat: a Pepperidge Farm cookie without chocolate is not a real Pepperidge Farm cookie. The popularity of the kind with molasses chips, oatmeal, sugaring, etc., may be taken as evidence of the decline of the West.

Fiat: adulteration of the chocolate essence rarely improves a P. Farm. Tahitis (chocolate plus coconut) and Nassaus (chocolate plus peanut) are very nice; Lidos (just chocolate) are better. We will, however, admit that the Mint Milano is superior to Milano *ordinaire*.

Fiat: the more chocolate the better. Hence the clear choice, the transcendental Pepperidge Farm cookie, the Geneva. The Geneva is not really a cookie at all, but a bittersweet chocolate bar with an edible, cookielike holder coated with crystallized sugar for enhanced textural contrast. There is no way to improve on the form.

THE BEST PIZZA

The Spot, 163 Wooster Street, New Haven. Texture is the key to superlative pizza. Most good pizzerias (for example, the Shakey's chain and Goldberg's in New York) distinguish themselves on flavor and foolishly accept the conventional up-from-Chef-Boy-Ar-Dee texture. At the Spot, the crust is thick and sinewy, imposing its presence on the chewer rather than meshing unassertively with the rest of the goop.

The Spot is a small, two-room restaurant tucked inconspicuously in the back of its own parking lot. It has a jukebox and three robust cats who warm themselves on the radiated heat of the pizza oven. On the wall is a poster blackened almost to invisibility by years of pizza ash. It has a picture of the Statue of Liberty and the legend "Loved by Millions. Joseph Schlitz Brewing Company. 1943."

THE BEST POLICE PRECINCT IN NEW YORK

If best means safest, the 123rd precinct—the southern third of Staten Island—ranks first. There your chances of being murdered in 1972 were nil; of being mugged, only 1 in 1,100. By contrast, 2 out of every 1,000 residents were murdered in Central Harlem and 62 out of every 1,000 reported being robbed on the street.

Excluding Staten Island—it is part of New York in name and taxes only—the safest precincts are the upper-middle-class 111th in Queens (1 murder per 100,000, 2½ muggings per 1,000) and the stable, lower-middle-class 62nd in Brooklyn (2 murders per 100,000, 2 muggings per 1,000). Unsurprisingly, the 19th precinct, the East Side between Fifty-ninth and Eighty-sixth streets, comes out best in Manhattan. But it is still three times as dangerous as the safe neighborhoods in Queens.

THE BEST PROPHECY

Philo T. Farnsworth, an inventor of television, demonstrated his success in 1927 for a financial backer, one George Everson. Among the crude images transmitted that day was a dollar sign. Said Everson afterward, "It seemed to jump out at us on the screen."

THE BEST PUT-DOWN OF A CRITIC

"I am sitting in the smallest room in my house. I have your review in front of me. Soon it will be behind me."

—Max Reger, a German composer

THE BEST RANDOM NUMBER TABLE

A *Million Random Digits with* 100,000 *Normal Deviates* by the RAND Corporation, beginning with "3174388901" and ending with "216847593." Some of the middle passages can be skipped.

THE BEST RATE OF RETURN ON STOCKHOLDERS' EQUITY, 1971

The Tobacco Industry—15.4 percent. It tells you something . . .

THE BEST-READ LAW CASE

Lason v. *State*, 12 So. 2d 305 (1943). This "dirty old man" case, read universally by first-year law students, resembles nothing so much as a 1949 smuggled version of Henry Miller. The binding of the reports volume at any law library is black with fingerprints and the book falls open automatically to the crucial page.

THE BEST RECORDING OF THE MESSIAH

Deutsche Grammophon (2709045). Conductor Karl Richter chooses the relatively austere eighteenth-century no-nonsense instrumentation for his London Philharmonic/John Alldis Choir recording. The soloists, particularly soprano Helen Donath and bass Donald McIntyre, are superb. But the most incredible aspect of the performance is the Richter sheen—the faultless integration of chorus, soloists, and orchestra, the clarity of the voices and instruments. It can be fancier, it can be louder, but it can't be better.

THE BEST RECORDINGS OF THE BEETHOVEN SYMPHONIES

Best Set: Concertgebouw Orchestra; Eugen Jochum, conductor; Netherlands Radio Chorus (Philips S-C71AX900). The famous von Karajan/Berlin Philharmonic (DG 2720007) and Klemperer/Philharmonia (Angel S-3619) are pedantic bores; the ancient NBC Orchestra/Toscanini is clearly the best, but the recordings are hopelessly inadequate for modern stereo equipment.

Best First: Concertgebouw/Jochum (Philips 6500087)—issued separately from the set.

Best Second: Cleveland Orchestra, George Szell (Columbia M7X-30281)—but it's available only as part of the set, and hardly worth the trouble for the recording, or the music.

Best Third: Philadelphia Orchestra, Eugene Ormandy (Columbia MS-6266)—romantic, though in this case it works.

Best Fourth: Philharmonia/Klemperer (Angel S-35661).

Best Fifth: Chicago Symphony Orchestra, Seiji Ozawa (RCA LSC-3132)—flashy, a shade undisciplined. Everything Leonard Bernstein's ought to have been.

Best Sixth: Chicago Symphony Orchestra, Fritz Reiner (RCA LSC-2614)—the sound engineering is dated, but Reiner is not.

Best Seventh: Vienna Philharmonic Orchestra, Georg Solti (London 6093)—simply wonderful; it would do Toscanini proud.

Best Eighth: Marlboro Festival Orchestra, Pablo Casals (Columbia MS-6931)—a more traditional alternative is the

Vienna Philharmonic Orchestra/Schmitt-Isserstedt (London CS6619).

Best Ninth: London Symphony Orchestra; Leopold Stokowski, conductor; London Symphony Chorus (soloists: Heather Harper, Helen Watts, Alexander Young, Donald McIntyre) (London 21043).

THE BEST REFUTATION OF THE MAXIM "YOU CAN'T TAKE IT WITH YOU"

Walter Winant, an American millionaire and sportsman, had £15,000 worth of great paintings tattooed on his back. Sotheby's has no plans to enter the market.

THE BEST RESORT HOTEL IN MEXICO

Las Brisas is hardly undiscovered. It is one of the most popular resorts in Acapulco and was named one of the three best hotels in the world by *Esquire*'s travel editor. Freshly debriefed astronauts unwind there with their families, courtesy of the ex-military American management.

But the beauty of Las Brisas is that its fame will cost you only money, not privacy. The hotel is a complex of hundreds of cottages built on terraces on a thousand-foot-high mountainside overlooking Acapulco Bay. Each "casita" is a self-contained environment. Each has a refrigerator stocked with fruit and drinks, most have their own tiny swimming pools heavily concealed from the outside by tropical shrubbery. Servants bring breakfast (and any other meal you wish) by jeep and change the hibiscus blossoms floating in the pool. Should you prefer company or strenuous exercise, Las Brisas maintains a beach club with two natural pools at the foot of the mountain.

THE BEST RESORT HOTEL IN THE CARIBBEAN

Most Caribbean hotels are designed for or by package-tour operators and the results are very dreary. At best, a well-managed Hilton where the chopped steak ordered medium-rare comes medium-rare. At worst, a dirty motel room with broken air conditioning and a pack of noisy eight-year-olds who seem to live in the swimming pool.

One of the most splendid exceptions is the Caneel Bay Plantation, St. John, a modest-sized complex spread over nearly a quarter square mile. Caneel Bay provides no excitement and little variety. Just understated luxury, excellent food, and privacy. There is plenty of beach on the property and miles of hiking in the contiguous national park. Boats are available for sailing, exploring, and scuba diving. The only drawback to this upper-middle-class paradise is that the clientele seem to have an average age of eighty-five. Younger Caribbean vacationers who can afford a place like Caneel Bay seem to prefer golf courses, casinos, and limbo dancers.

A virtually identical experience can be had at Little Dix

Bay on Virgin Gorda in the British Virgin Islands: quiet luxury, good food and service, a beach. The similarity is not a coincidence. Both were created to suit the vanity of their owner, Laurance Rockefeller, whose hobby has grown into the most sophisticated of resort chains, Rockresorts, Inc.

THE BEST RESTAURANT IN PARIS

The French food establishment is fond of proclaiming the ruin of *haute cuisine*. Cooking in the grand manner, so the theory goes, cannot withstand the intense commercialism and striving middle-class mentality of modern city life. In Paris the signs are everywhere: Les Halles, the great central market, has been exiled to the sticks to make room for parking lots and office buildings; suburbanites pass up traditional bistros in favor of restaurants devoted to steak and shish kebab; the busiest spot on the Champs-Elysées at lunchtime is McDonald's.

We cannot agree. It is true that the seven-course, two-hour lunch is on the wane—Parisians have neither the time nor the death wish to consume 2,500 calories of butterfat in the middle of the day. But quantity is not quality. The discipline of small meals has, if anything, raised the standard of classic cuisine. And choosing the best restaurant is still the most pleasurable (though perhaps arbitrary) task imaginable.

Where to begin? The last decade has seen an explosion of restaurants practicing brilliant variations on old themes:

Archestrate, the tiny restaurant of Alain Senderens that has dared to serve such perversities as garlic-free snails, lobster with peaches, and essence-of-rose soufflé; Lamazère, perhaps the most expensive table in France, thanks to the unrestricted use of truffles and fresh foie gras; Vivarois, a restaurant that did not exist in 1965, yet earned a third Michelin star in 1973; Le Pot au Feu, Michel Guérard's hole-in-the-wall amid suburban warehouses, which has won the cognoscenti with simple inventions like artichoke salad with foie gras.

But our own conservative tastes lead us back to the palaces of elegance and discretion. Some of the most famous are showing the wear of decades of publicity and uncomplaining tourists—the Tour d'Argent and Lapérouse to name two. Maxim's is Maxim's, a happening, not a restaurant. Still, most are nearly perfect—Lasserre, in spite of the feeling of being on the Hollywood set of a French restaurant; Lucas-Carton and Taillevent, houses of tradition that inexplicably escape fame.

Our choice, if only for its ultimate professionalism, is Grand Vefour. Vefour might have gone the way of Maxim's —the name, if not the quality, has been marketed abroad, and the owner, Raymond Oliver, has become a cookbook entrepreneur and television personality—but it hasn't. Vefour is for serious eaters. The waiters do not fawn (neither do they sneer); the wines are expertly chosen and stored; the *grands plats* are served without benefit of lard sculpture or neon light. Specialties include toast de crevettes Rothschild—a brioche box filled with tiny shrimp in a dense sauce; pigeon stuffed with foie gras and sausage; lamprey eel, a conceit chosen solely as a vehicle for the richest of sauces Bordelaises; chocolate soufflé that is deliberately overloaded with chocolate and undercooked to simulate a hot custard crowned by egg crust. If the cuisine at Le Grand Vefour has declined, the descent has escaped our observation. The only intrusion of the New Europe is on the bill—about forty dollars per person.

THE BEST RESTAURANT IN PENNSYLVANIA

Pennsylvania's great cities, Philadelphia and Pittsburgh, are not known for their fine cuisine. When the Mellons and the Pughs eat out, they dine in corporate board rooms or private clubs. Joe's, however, is special. It is not only the best restaurant in Pennsylvania, but a fine restaurant by any standard. Visitors to this rather undistinguished-looking eating place in a rather undistinguished mill town (Reading) will discover a sophisticated menu dedicated to the celebration of the mushroom. The owner and chef, mushroom enthusiast Joe Czarnecki, has managed to incorporate the fungus in about half of his dishes. The wild mushroom soup is remarkable, as is the mushroom-scented filet mignon. Joe's wine list suffers from the indifference of Pennsylvania's state alcohol monopoly, but suffices.

THE BEST ROOSEVELT LINE

"I have a simple philosophy. Fill what's empty, empty what's full, and scratch where it itches."

—Alice Roosevelt Longworth

THE BEST SACHER TORTE

SBy too many criteria Vienna is just a second-rate Paris, a little calmer, much quieter perhaps, but dumpy and lead-footed, the capital of an empire that was senile long before its death. On one count, however, Vienna can hold its own: pastry. Coffee and cake are still a way of life in the city, and the most Viennese of all cake is the Sacher torte—a chocolate sponge base coated with apricot jam and then iced with sugary dark chocolate. The flavor of the combination is so intense and unbalanced toward carbohydrate that the traditional whipped cream accompaniment serves to moderate rather than accentuate its excess.

Dozens of bakeries and coffeehouses sell Sacher torte, but only one, the Café Sacher, is legally entitled to vend the "genuine" Sacher torte. That right was established after a court fight with Demel's coffeehouse, which had purchased the recipe from a philistine Sacher heir in the not distant past. Of course it doesn't make much difference what the magistrates said, taste is what counts, and all that Demel's was forced to change was the claim on their chocolate seal stamped on each cake.

Now Demel's was, and is, the most famous bakery in the

world. Food writer Joseph Wechsberg recounts that even Fernand Point, the founder of the faith of modern French cuisine, acknowledged its supremacy. From humble origins as one of hundreds of sweet shops in mid-nineteenth-century Vienna, Demel's empire flourished while the Hapsburgs' withered. All the middle-European tortes are on occasion available, along with the most decadent of chocolate and marzipan creations in season. Pick any day of the year and you will find the coffeehouse jammed with celebrants waiting patiently for their turns at the marble display counter. Thus it is not surprising that the same critics who find Demel's strudel better than the Hungarian original have pronounced Demel's Sacher torte better than the copyright holder's.

We do not agree. The Café Sacher makes a superior version. The difference is not one of freshness or baking skill, but one of conception. The Café Sacher splits the spongecake and separates the layers with apricot, while Demel's only glazes the surface. More important, the Café Sacher employs a tarter apricot mix and a thicker shell of chocolate. Such distinctions might appear trivial, but the net effect is striking. Demel's Sacher torte reflects the imbalance of ingredients all too well—it seems a poor man's torte, lacking the requisite butterfat. The Café Sacher's version transforms vice to virtue—the cake calling forth comparisons with hideously rich candy rather than some lesser family of pastry.

THE BEST SCIENCE FICTION NOVEL

Science fiction is not literature—even to pose the question is to betray the medium. Nobody demands literature from Agatha Christie or Dashiell Hammett. It's all that insecure fretting by English majors and earnest biochemists who need an excuse to escape reading *Commentary* in their spare time. Imaginative trash by A. E. Van Vogt or James Blish gets snubbed, while Ray Bradbury's I-spent-the-summer-at-the-Bread-Loaf-Writers'-Conference prose is compared to Melville's. Unfavorably, of course; SF *poseurs* aren't idiots.

Real science fiction usually comes in one of two packages:

—Novels like Frank Herbert's *Dune* or Isaac Asimov's *Foundation,* in which future civilizations are constructed; much attention to detail, some plot, little characterization. The fun is in the technology/sociology. One can even spot some irony.

—Space operas, like Robert Heinlein's *The Moon Is a Harsh Mistress.* These are conventional escapist novels in an unusual setting. Romance at the Venus Spaceport instead of by the pool in Marrakech. Heinlein's books, incidentally, are marred by heavy doses of right-wing political philosophy. Better, though, than run-of-the-mill pseudo-*1984*'s.

Our favorite—if you can find it—Alfred Bester's *The Stars of My Destination,* scrimps on neither side. It is exciting nonsense about a semiliterate technician trapped in a disabled spacecraft who discovers education and saves himself. Then comes an immensely complicated and very satisfying plot about rescuing the secret of an explosive that can be detonated by thought waves, and other goodies. There's a moral—several in fact—but nothing profound enough to mess up the story.

THE BEST SEVEN-LETTER WORD FOR SCRABBLE

$$J_8 O_1 N_1 Q_{10} U_1 I_1 L_1$$

or, using a blank,

$$Q_{10} U_1 I_1 Z_{10} [\quad] E_1 R_1$$

THE BEST SHOTGUN

The common hardware-store shotgun has regal cousins. The best of these are custom-made—or more precisely, custom-modified—weapons finished from factory-machined parts.

Custom work can include a redesigned stock made to the specifications of the owner from Circassian walnut (preserved with oil rather than epoxy), a choice of trigger actions, special curing or "bluing" of the barrels, and super-precise hand-finishing of the internal parts. Often a substantial fraction of the custom input consists of elaborate but nonfunctional gold and silver inlays in the gun's receiver. The few remaining gunsmiths who accept commissions for such work will charge at least $3,000 for their services.

A satisfactory alternative is to buy one of the elite factory shotguns made for field, skeet, or trap, and pay an extra $1,000 or so for special hand-finishing. Traditionalists—mostly the British—seem to prefer the double-barrel, side-by-side configuration. Something on the order of the Harrington and Richardson Webley-Scott 700 series, which sells in the $1,000-plus range. A majority of purchasers of expensive guns, particularly on the Continent, use the over/under two-barrel configuration. The O/U combination is more aesthetic and potentially more accurate, though technically difficult to align. Hence the higher prices. Here the best is the famous Belgian Browning Superposed, which can run about $1,500 in optional finishes.

The most elegant shotguns of all are the automatics. There is no need for a second barrel, since the gun automatically reloads like an automatic rifle. North American bird hunters are limited to a three-shot magazine, though five-shot magazines are standard. Probably the best of these lightweight shotguns is the Italian Franchi. Its Imperial grade with hand-fitted parts and gold inlay design weighs only six pounds with a twelve-gauge barrel, and it can be had for less than $2,000.

THE BEST SKI

Big money, rapidly changing technology, and sophisticated Madison Avenue packaging have turned skiing into a consumer's fantasy/nightmare. Ponder the choice available. At least two hundred models, produced by thirty manufacturers from eight countries, are sold in the United States. The simple metal and wood sandwich construction that dominated the industry ten years ago has given way to a dazzling variety of designs—metal/fiberglass, fiberglass/foam, fiberglass/epoxy, fiberglass/wood, etc.

Ski magazines are little help. Their equipment reviews, like those in photography, automobile, and stereo publications, are masterworks of diplomacy: no falsehoods, but not much assistance in choosing between the products of actual or potential advertisers.

Fortunately, most expensive skis are very, very good. Better than anything Jean Claude Killy used ten years ago. The only trick is to match the model and size to the ability of the skier and type of snow. Weekend skiers need skis that turn easily at low speeds; more demanding skiers need longer, stiffer skis that suppress vibration at high speeds and permit modern sit-back turns. The best ski on ice will not be the best ski in deep powder—the former requires super vibration dampening and "cracked" edges; the latter, a very soft flex.

Probably the most versatile ski for the good to excellent skier—beginners would be wasting their money—is the fiberglass/wood Dynamic VR17. Dynamic is a small French manufacturer that briefly and unhappily experimented with an American-made ski to be marketed by Lange. Dynamic went home in 1972 and is once more producing the Ferrari of the industry—semitraditional engineering, state-of-the-art durability and performance.

THE BEST SKI BINDING

Skiing is a very dangerous sport. Accidents are rarely fatal —save those of downhill racers who crack up at seventy miles an hour. But a really amazing number of skiers, tens of thousands each year, suffer severe sprains, knee cartilage damage, and complicated leg fractures. The overwhelming cause of these injuries is binding failure.

Bindings usually fail because they are improperly adjusted or fouled with grit. The percentage of skiers who take even the most elementary precautions is no higher than the percentage of drivers who wear shoulder belts. Part of the problem, however, is that no perfect binding exists. As simple as they appear, bindings perform very complex functions. Obviously, a well-engineered binding must release the boot from the ski before sufficent force is applied to the foot to damage something. Yet that force may come from virtually any angle. To complicate matters, a premature release may be just as dangerous as no release at all. The better the skier, the more shock the binding must routinely tolerate without release. Racers and aggressive skiers are ultimately forced to compromise between the symmetric risks of too little and too much protection.

Probably the most successful binding design to date is the Spademan. Spademan's has no toepiece—the binding connection is on the sole of the boot—thereby simplifying the dynamics of release in a forward fall. Other manufacturers, notably Gertsch, Besser, Burt, Americana, and Head, have new plate-type designs with similar advantages. Most big ski schools now use the Spademan on their Graduated Length Method rental equipment. The binding can be pre-set for the weight of the skier rather than for the idiosyncrasies of the individual boot. More important, the Spademan is particularly effective in the common slow-speed fall; these bindings have cut injuries by about 25 percent among beginners.

Spademan bindings may be nearly perfect for novices, but most experts remain unconverted, on the theory that the Spademan does not have the shock-absorption capacity of more traditional designs. Racers, a paradoxically conservative breed, largely stick with the French Look/Nevada heel and toe combination, the first of the really effective shock-absorbing bindings. Top-of-the-line equipment made by Geze, Salomon, Marker, and Rosemount is no doubt just as good. And all of these traditional-design bindings can be made more effective with mechanical anti-friction devices. Plates with Teflon bearings, like the Rosemount Lotork, virtually eliminate binding failure due to friction between the boot and ski.

THE BEST SKI BOOTS

Modern ski boots are ugly and uncomfortable. They are nearly impossible to walk in, difficult to fit, and grotesquely expensive. Yet without them great skiers would be mediocre and mediocre skiers would be unable to make parallel turns.

The purpose of the ski boot is to weld the leg to the ski so that a shift in weight is precisely translated into a change in weight and angle at which the skis bite the snow. Good boots—almost all boots—have rigid shells of plastic or fiberglass, rather than leather, to facilitate precision ski-edge control. For the same reason, massive pressure buckles have replaced laces; modern boots hold the foot like a vice. Of course, this unnatural foot covering hurts. Imagine an ordinary pair of shoes made of plastic. Hence the ingenious efforts to pad the inside of the boot without reducing the rigid hold. The most expensive boots are custom-fitted by filling in the space around the foot with plastic foam. When it works, it's the best, but it often doesn't. Head and a number of others employ air bladders that are pumped up by hand each time you ski.

A conservative alternative is to use boots with silicone-filled capsules (the kind Carol Doda made famous), which mold under pressure and heat to the shape of your foot. The Lange Phantom, a product of the company that started the plastic boot revolution, is as good as any. We suspect, however, the boot of the future is the Scott. Scott makes the best and most expensive ski poles. Now it manufactures a super-thin plastic boot that weighs only half as much as the competition, opens from the rear, fastens with a single buckle, and permits adjustment in forward lean and degree of forward flexibility.

THE BEST SKI RESORT IN EUROPE

If you want the best snow in the world, go to Utah. To avoid endless lift lines and teenagers unacquainted with the Golden Rule, try the Canadian Rockies. But if what you really have in mind is skiing with style, nothing compares with Europe.

Which ski area is best depends on what you have really come for. The best skiing for experts is probably at Val-d'Isère or Chamonix. Val's demanding slopes may have the most dependable snow in the Alps; Chamonix offers vertical drops of a mile and a half and a ten-mile excursion down the Vallée Blanche. And if the two-hour wait for the cable car gets you down, you can always make a pilgrimage to the eating country around Lyons in less than a day.

For skiers in search of simpler bourgeois virtues, the fine variety and sunny, open slopes of Austria's Lech may be right; what Lech cannot provide, nearby Zürs and St. Anton can. For those who detest the economic anarchy that has turned many French and Austrian resorts into traffic-choked commercial monstrosities, the planned comforts of Marcel Breuer-designed Flaine may suit. Flaine doesn't have the very best skiing, but it is good enough. And a guest will glimpse neither automobile nor ersatz Swiss chalet for the entire stay.

Our own choice is Zermatt. Thanks to high altitude, Zermatt has a long, dependable skiing season that extends into the summer on the glacier. It provides incredible terrain variety on four interconnected mountains, including an endless run down the Italian side of the Matterhorn to Cervinia. The village itself may no longer be picturesque but does protect the citizenry from incursions by the automobile. None of Zermatt's hotels compares favorably with St.-Moritz's ultra-fashionable Palace, nor do its restaurants with Mégève's Michelin-starred La Gérentière, but you will not go sleepless or hungry.

THE BEST SKYSCRAPER

You might quibble with the name of the category, but there has to be a place in *The Best* for New York's Flatiron Building. Designed by D. H. Burnham in 1902, the triangular office building stands today as ironic testimony to the promise of modern architecture, largely unrealized seven decades later.

As one drives down Broadway, the Flatiron presents a dramatic angular façade, a lean delicacy that moves the viewer to ponder the miracle of its structural integrity. Partly that delicacy is achieved quite conventionally: the pleasingly detailed limestone façade creates a light and airy mood. Partly it is a clever, intellectual trick. While Renaissance Revival architecture ordinarily imparts a solid feeling by forcing the eye downward, the horizontal lines here emphasize the angular perspective. The Flatiron looks as if it is about to take off, or at very least cut a great trench between the diagonal avenues.

THE BEST SPORTS CAR UNDER $7,000

Sports cars in this price range usually compromise design characteristics. Tight handling and decent acceleration are expensive to build into a low-volume automobile that must go three thousand miles between tune-ups. (The $6,000 Porsches—the 914 and the out-of-production 912—are incapable of dragging a Plymouth Duster.) The British-engineered Lotus is an exception: four-wheel independent suspension, rack-and-pinion steering, and disk brakes provide racing-quality handling. A twin overhead cam, four-cylinder 1500 cc engine manages 113 horsepower. That's enough to propel the light chassis and fiberglass body from 0 to 60 in seven seconds, 0 to 100 in twenty. Top speed, 120 mph.

The Elan is comfortable enough, though short on frills. For a modest sacrifice in performance and another $1,000 you can have the Elan Plus Two, with sleeker body style, more luxurious finishing, and a vestigial back seat. The Plus Two has had much to recommend it since Lotus stopped exporting the coupe model of the Elan in favor of the vaguely awkward-looking convertible.

One major disadvantage of the Elan is servicing. Dealers are hard to find outside big cities, and the fiberglass body that keeps the list price down and the acceleration up is extremely difficult to repair. A possible alternative might be the Datsun 240Z. Not quite the Lotus in performance, but far more muscular than the competition. Some people even like its up-from-Corvette, toughest-car-on-the-block body style.

THE BEST STEAKHOUSE IN CHICAGO

For some reason people believe that the best steak comes from the places where cattle are slaughtered. The best meat does spend some time there, but since the invention of the refrigerated rail car, outsiders have had no difficulty in capturing a fair portion.

Still, Chicago (which incidentally no longer has stock-yards) does have fine steakhouses. The best is Don Roth's Blackhawk in the Loop. All the steaks are USDA Prime (not in itself a guarantee of quality), all are aged and cut thick. There is much controversy over how to cook such slabs. The Blackhawk starts them over an open fire and then finishes off the thickest under a broiler.

THE BEST STEREO FOR ABOUT $500

The electronic hardware in stereo equipment is usually not expensive in its own right; what costs is design research. Hence sophisticated engineering usually trickles down, once the manufacturer exploits the luxury market to the limits—or other firms rush in with copies. $500 buys more sound now than $1,000 would have bought a decade ago. Our system on a budget:

—The Sherwood S-7200 AM/FM receiver ($250, discounted). There are lots of adequate receivers in this price range. The S-7200 is special because it has a very muscular amplifier—forty watts per channel—yet does not cut any crucial corners on the tuner section.

—The AR manual turntable ($70, discounted), the turntable of choice for systems twice as expensive. It isn't sexy, but it is accurate, quiet, and dependable.

—The Shure 91E cartridge ($17, discounted). Everybody makes good cartridges these days. This one tracks at 1.5 grams and would probably be the strongest link in any conceivable sound system under $1,000.

—The Bose 501 Series II speakers ($225/pair, discounted).
These are the cheapest omnidirectional speakers meant for
serious listening. Of course, Bose 901's are better, but at
$500 a pair, they are out of range.

THE BEST STEREO FOR $1,000

STRATEGY A: NO-COMPROMISE SOUND
Scrap the idea of an FM tuner and substitute a simple turntable for an automatic changer. Stereo tuners with fine
signal resolution and noise-reduction systems are very expensive—anything less than the best means a sacrifice when
fine component speakers and amplifier are added. Automatic changers are $100 more expensive than equally ac-
curate turntables. Besides, changers are bad for the records.

Match an Integral Systems Model 200U amplifier ($200)
with an Integral Systems Model 10 preamp ($240) for the
cleanest 200 watts imaginable. Add an AR manual turntable ($70, discounted) and an ADC–XLM cartridge ($29,
discounted)—a combination with a performance only a
shade off $300 units. That leaves almost enough—we'll cheat
a little—for a pair of Bose 901 Series II speakers ($500), the
purest sound source imaginable at anywhere near the price.

STRATEGY B: CONVENIENCE COUNTS
In place of the manual turntable, substitute the Benjamin/
Miracord 50H ($150, discounted), keeping the ADC–XLM
cartridge. The 50H is nearly as good as the much more
popular Dual 1229, and is $50 cheaper. If you did well in
high school shop, far and away the best receiver is the 180-

watt Heathkit AR-1500 ($400). For an extra $250 Heath is willing to assemble it—a marketing strategy that should be investigated by Bess Myerson, since assembly costs the company only another $10 or $15. If you can't manage the kit, you will have to settle for the perfectly acceptable 120-watt Pioneer SX-828 receiver ($400, discounted). There's no reason to deviate from the choice of Bose 901 Series II speakers.

THE BEST STEREO SYSTEM AT ANY PRICE

High-quality sound reproduction is getting cheaper, but the best is still enough to keep an average neurosurgeon cutting overtime. The true stereo freak has become a quadraphonic freak—double your pleasure, double your price; in truth, stereo is still better.

At the heart of any system is the amplifier/preamp/tuner. It's convenient to buy them together, as a receiver, and the finest receiver around is the Marantz 19 ($1,200). For the dedicated, however, convenience is not the name of the game. Big receivers just don't deliver enough power to get optimum performance from the new-generation speakers; FM tuners have also passed the Marantz in sophistication. We would match an Integral Systems Model 1000 amplifier ($1,000) delivering, you guessed it, 1,000 watts, with an Integral Systems Model 20X preamp ($500) that uses the new compressor/expander technology to suppress noise from virtually any source. For those who would rather wait, Kenwood is said to be developing a

2,000-watt integrated amp/preamp. The finest FM tuner available is the Sequerra ($1,600), complete with a digital readout instead of a dial, Dolby Noise Reduction, and oscilloscope displays for anything you might want to know, and plenty of other things you wouldn't dream of asking. Sony is expected to offer a similar unit for about $1,200, while Heath has a less spectacular digital readout tuner in kit form for a mere $600.

By comparison, state-of-the-art turntables are almost free. Technic's SL1100A ($350) is as good as any: along with the usual refinements, it has a platter driven directly by the motor that uses solid-state control circuitry to maintain a uniform speed over line voltage fluctuations. The etched aluminum SL1100A, incidentally, is also the most beautiful turntable around. On sheer technical pizzazz nothing matches one alternative, Bang and Olufsen's new Beogram 4000 ($500)—a photo sensor scans the records, then chooses the appropriate speed. For the SL1100A, you would probably want the Shure V-15 Type III cartridge ($60, discounted), capable of tracking at 0.6 grams with minimal distortion over the audible frequencies. The Technic tone arm is first rate, though you could replace it with the ultimate—a Shure SME 3012.

Purists prefer tapes to discs. Besides the advantage of uninterrupted play and less exposure to damage, magnetic tape can be a more faithful reproducer of sound. Until quite recently, though, tape cassettes were dramatically inferior to the reel-to-reel variety—background hiss and distortion made cassette use pointless with quality amplifiers and speakers.

The Japanese Nakamichi 1000 ($1,100) changed all that.

It is probably not superior to the best tape decks (say, a Tandberg 9000X), but it comes close enough. Electronic cuing circuitry phases in each sub-system when you start the machine, eliminating all initial distortion; separate record and playback heads let you hear what you are recording, while you are recording. Two noise-reduction systems (Dolby B and DNL) can be used on the playback mode.

The quality of an amplifier or a cassette deck or a turntable is a matter of numbers—how accurate are they, under what conditions? Not so the speaker. Numbers surely count, but the ultimate pleasure of sound defies precise quantification. Ten different speakers that are equal on paper will each sound different. The same speaker will sound different in different rooms, or with different placement in the same room. Not surprisingly then, speaker design is the wildest frontier in audio equipment design; at the moment there is a definite bias toward crazy (and ugly). Multidirectional speakers that use interior baffles and room walls as sounding boards are in fashion: big, low-frequency woofers combined with a half-dozen or more small, high-frequency tweeters in a single enclosure. Audioanalyst's Pyramedia ($575 each) looks like a pyramid; the EPI Tower ($1,000 each) is an eight-foot column; the Ohm F ($400 each) is a ringer for a circa-1926 Frigidaire. We'll stick with the AR-LST ($600 each), a hybrid of Acoustic Research's sweet, sweet Model 3a. The nine speakers per unit can tolerate, even benefit from, vast power sources, though the instruction manual solemnly warns against surges greater than 1,000 watts. A nice gimmick is a six-way switch that permits instant changes from one preprogrammed internal speaker balance to another—in essence, a switch that lets you match the speakers to your mood.

Of course, if you want to listen alone, there's a cheaper solution. The sound from Koss ESP-9 Electrostatic Headphones ($150) is nearly perfect: an acoustically accurate pseudoreality that you may find to be better than the real thing.

THE BEST STRATEGY FOR BUYING LIFE INSURANCE

Straight life insurance is Newspeak for life insurance plus forced savings. Part of the premium insures your life—it's a bet between you and the company, a bet that everyone hopes will be won by the company. The other part goes into an account that pays dividends (read interest) at some guaranteed rate. Term insurance is just life insurance—cash on the gravestone, period.

Since most people really want only insurance when they buy insurance, term has its virtues. Nobody requires you to purchase two light bulbs with every pound of ground chuck—why mix savings and life insurance? The argument becomes particularly compelling when you look at the return on straight life. Life insurance companies have conservative investment policies and greedy stockholders, and advertise a lot. Insurance agents have to eat too—usually 55 percent of the first year's premium. After expenses are paid, there is precious little left over for dividends.

Buying term, incidentally, is not as easy as buying ground

117

chuck. Insurance is such a complicated business and people are so cowed by agents that different companies can get away with widely varying prices for the same policy. Rule number one is to avoid personalized service from an independent agent. He usually has nothing to offer beyond an hour of Rotary Club chatter, and it can be an expensive hour. Policies written through groups—unions, churches, etc.—often have the least fat added to the premium. Next best is insurance sold over the counter by savings banks, but it's not available in most states because of the power of the insurance lobby. Otherwise, shop around.

Straight life still may be marginally preferable to term for people in high tax brackets. Attractively priced straight life—there is even more variation here than in term—will return about 5 percent on the investment portion. That's no better than most savings accounts and a lot worse than other safe ways to save. But, in its infinite wisdom, the Congress has chosen to sweeten the pot. Dividends deducted from premiums are not taxable. If you are in a very high bracket, a guaranteed 5 percent, plus immunity from the IRS, could be a fair deal. It probably isn't, though, for most people rich enough to care—insurance is not the only tax shelter, after all. Besides, returns as high as 5 percent depend on holding the policy in force for about fifteen years. Companies swallow an enormous chunk of the first few years' premiums, for expenses, and it takes a long time to catch up.

The insurance industry's answer to these arguments, or more precisely, to consumer resistance to $1,500 premiums, is a hybrid called minimum deposit plan insurance. You

118

pay one or two regular premiums, then you borrow from the cash value of the policy to pay future premiums. That sounds like double-talk, but it isn't. In effect all you are really doing is buying a fancy form of term insurance. Some agents claim that minimum deposit actually works out cheaper than ordinary term insurance—the companies, it seems, are hoping you will revert to straight life and they take a chance in order to get your business. Maybe, but probably not. Ninety-nine out of one hundred agents don't understand much more about insurance than the size of their commissions, and minimum deposit is a lot more profitable than selling term policies.

THE BEST STRATEGY FOR INVESTING IN THE STOCK MARKET

Rule No. 1: A Broker Can't Help.
Look closely, and you will see that your broker is the kid who got a B— by copying "igneous" off your final exam in freshman geology. If he is a smart broker, he spelled it right and got an A—.

Call your broker for advice and he will read to you from the List of Recommended Stocks, hot from the research department's time-sharing terminal. The list is so hot that only today has it been made available to the firm's 68,000 private clients, and only last week did their forty-odd institutional clients—pension funds, bank trust departments, and whatnot—get a first peek. Peddling stock is a tough business, especially in these troubled times. And chances are your broker knows less about it than Mr. Kiplinger at *Changing Times*. If he did know something, why would he give it away for a lousy sixty-dollar commission?

Rule No. 2: Play for the Fast Buck, and the Odds Are Ferocious.

In a good year, the market goes up maybe 30 percent; in a bad year it will go down about that much. Even if you are bullish about America, the most you can hope for in the

long pull is to stay 7 or 8 percent ahead of inflation. Now, every time you buy and sell a stock, the round trip costs 2 or 3 percent. Churn the old portfolio five times a year, and there goes 10 to 15 percent of your capital. You might discover Xerox on the way up, but it won't make much difference if you sell it in two months. In Las Vegas, at least, they give you Ann-Margret and free drinks to ease the pain.

Rule No. 3: Most Systems Don't Work. The Ones That Do, Don't Work for Long.

The system with the most advocates that has been around the longest is called Chartism. A Chartist searches for patterns in bar graphs of the day-to-day movement of stock prices. True Believers are all mystics—they show touching faith in icons like the Head and Shoulders pattern and a remarkable resistance to statistical inference. Unfortunately, no theory of stock price movements seems to work better than the nihilistic Random Walk: every day is a new dawn; the past has no influence on the future. Even if the Random Walkers are wrong, the patterns must be too small to take advantage of, if you are paying retail commissions. Remember about churning . . .

One system that did work involved purchasing stock while simultaneously selling short warrants, issued on the same stock, due to expire within a few months. Since warrants generally sell at a premium above their actual worth, they have to go down relative to the price of the stock. Heads you win, tails you win.

If you didn't follow that, no matter. Enough people did understand it to wipe out the entire potential gain—all the premiums odd-lot suckers paid for those warrants in the first place. There is a lesson here, though. Not only must you discover a system that works—an exploitable irrationality in stock prices—in order to make money, you must be one of the first to discover it.

Rule No. 4: Mutual Funds Are Not the Answer.

The answer, perhaps. But not the Answer. What they can do is save the hassle of trying to diversify a small nest egg. Ten or twenty thousand doesn't buy many round lots of blue, or even aqua, chips, and those commissions on odd-lot trading can kill you. The trick is to purchase closed-end funds on the stock exchange, or avoid a broker altogether and pick up no-load mutuals directly from the management. If you buy a mutual fund from a brokerage house, the first 8.5 percent is commission—how else did you think the salesmen pay for their double-knit suits? That 8.5 percent buys you exactly nothing; no-loads perform just as well as their rip-off cousins.

What a mutual can't do is make you rich if you didn't start out that way. Diversification cuts both ways. No fund manager, no matter how smart, consistently picks winners. In a bull market a fund may do very well, but the odds against it doing very, very well are high. The hottest mutual fund of all, Rowe Price New Horizons, averaged 13 percent from 1962 to 1972 while Standard and Poor's 500 stock index managed a respectable 6. The second-best mutual fund averaged 11, the third-best, only 9.

One way of changing that arithmetic is to buy a fund that concentrates in a single industry: less diversification, more risk. But then you might as well buy a few stocks on your own. Open-end funds face another problem. When the market is high, everybody wants in—the funds are swimming in cash, but there are no bargains in sight. When the market is low, solid stocks may offer a 20 percent return, but the funds have no money to buy them.

For the big mutuals, it's even worse. Say some anal-retentive Wharton MBA in the research department discovers a nifty little ski binding company that may be the next Polaroid. Trouble is, a purchase of as little as a half million dollars of the closely held stock will drive its price up ten points. But what is $500,000 for a mutual fund that must find a way to invest $200 million? It is no coincidence that in a sample of fourteen no-load funds, eight didn't do as well during the 1960's as the S & P 500.

Rule No. 5: Fundamentals Are Boring. Anything Else Is Shooting Craps.
There is a way to make a lot of money in the market; however, it is the same as the way to lose a lot of money in the market. Since this is such an obvious point, why does each investor believe, deep down inside, he is above the law of large numbers? One must invoke the psychological principle of partial reinforcement. A pigeon that receives a kernel of corn each time it pecks a button quickly loses interest in the game if the kernels stop coming. But a pigeon that randomly receives a kernel every seventh or eighth peck will keep pecking futilely for hours after the corn is cut off.

The only remotely sensible strategy for choosing stocks is to look for solid companies in industries with no serious clouds in the future. Then buy when the price-earnings ratios seem unreasonably low and sell when the price-earnings ratios seem unreasonably high. Of course, it doesn't always work. IBM facing an anti-trust suit might end up a better investment at 100:1 than Borg-Warner at 6:1, after the fact. But then, nothing always works.

THE BEST STRATEGY FOR INVESTING
IN WINE

A decade ago, vintage wine was a dynamite investment. Better than double eagles, Picasso ceramics, or antique Bokharas. Almost as good as Xerox or MGIC, and much more dependable from year to year. Château Lafite-Rothschild '59 could be had in 1962 for less than $5. Today you are lucky to find a case for less than $1,000. The few remaining bottles of long-lived, first-growth Bordeaux of pre–World War II vintages fetch whatever the New Money thinks they are worth—$9,600 recently for a jeroboam (four-bottle size) of Château Mouton-Rothschild '29. Even wines lacking that magic last name have done pretty well: Château Haut-Brion '55 has appreciated 1,200 percent since it first left the cellars.

Like all good investments you didn't make, wine was a natural. Demand can only go up—unless you think the middle classes will lose their taste for alcohol and status. But supply is virtually fixed—Château Latour does not grow on trees, only on vines, very particular vines. A highly rated estate would need ten to twenty years to expand without debasing the output. Besides, there are compensations if you guess wrong. It isn't like losing on the commodity futures market and getting a carload of pork bellies COD at the back door.

There are, however, as they say in those prospectuses filed with the SEC, problems. Lots and lots of people agree wine is a good investment. That's great if you already own some choice acreage in St.-Estèphe, but not so great if you are bidding at the wine auctions. An infant bottle of Château Mouton-Rothschild may run $40. Say storage and insurance are 2 percent a year and you figure a net return of less than 12 percent wouldn't make the gamble attractive. Mouton is virtually undrinkable for the first five or ten years and only nears its peak after twenty. If you wait the full twenty years to sell, a $40 bottle will have to be worth $650 to make the investment worthwhile. Maybe a dozen Texas millionaires and publicity-hungry wine retailers are paying that kind of money for Mouton in its prime; will there be enough to absorb the few hundred cases that still might be around?

The odds are better on fine classified clarets like Château Léoville-Las-Cases, or Great Growth Burgundies like Charmes-Chambertin, currently selling in their youth for $7. Other problems, however, intervene. Few wine brokers in France are willing to act as agents for small investors. London wine dealers do perform the function, but the costs are high. Some New York and San Francisco merchants who are their own wholesalers have also been known to make an arrangement for a good customer, though, again, it will cost.

You could always buy a hundred cases from the local liquor store and stack them up in the cellar. The cellar, however, had better be cold (45 to 55 degrees), dark, and not very damp. Red wine cannot age properly in a closet; it may, in fact, spoil after a year or two at room temperature. And once the investment is ready to liquidate, state authorities, acting on behalf of those public-spirited wine distributors who remember them at Christmas, may be reluctant to grant permission.

THE BEST STRAWBERRY PRESERVES

Supermarket mush labeled strawberry preserves is for small children and Wonder Bread. Far too much sugar and preservative, too little strawberry flavor. One reasonable alternative is the honest product of Hero, the Swiss jam manufacturer. To our taste it is still too sweet. A most prestigious and expensive candidate is Tiptree's Little Scarlet. Tiptree's is conservative with sugar and loaded with fruit, but has a rather odd unvarying consistency. The preserve is an almost uniform paste with no pleasing contrast between berry and syrup.

Our candidate for the best is Dickenson's Fancy Preserves. Dickenson's is the platonic form of strawberry preserves. It looks like the stuff we grew up on, but owes not a molecule of strawberry flavor to the good works of New Jersey's petrochemical industry. The berries are barely cooked, the syrup unburdened with pectin, the mixture a neat balance of acid and sweet.

THE BEST SUMMATION OF OXFORD PHILOSOPHY

"We are about to watch, from seats high up at the back of the stadium, a football match in which one of the teams is

126

Japanese. One of the teams comes running into the arena. I might say,

(1) 'They look like ants'; or
(2) 'They look like Europeans.'

Now it is plain enough that in saying (1), I do *not* mean either that I am inclined to think that some ants have come on to the field, or that the players, on inspection, would be found to look exactly, or even rather, like ants. (I may know quite well, and even be able to see, that for instance they haven't got that very striking sort of nipped-in waist.)"

—J. L. Austin, *Sense and Sensibilia*

THE BEST SUNTAN LOTION

Suntan-lotion advertising is blatantly fraudulent. No cream or gel or foam or butter can make you tan any faster than you would *au naturel*. Quite the contrary. The only active ingredients in suntan preparations are chemicals that block the absorption of ultraviolet radiation. They simply slow down the whole process.

Nor can suntan lotion promote tan while preventing burn. There is a difference between tanning and burning rays. But the sunscreen chemicals are equally effective in inhibiting both. Hence the most you can expect is a little protection against self-indulgence. If you try to tan too quickly, the result is a burn that destroys a layer of skin and forces you to start again from the beginning many painful days later. Good suntan lotion gives you extra time in the sun without a burn (or a tan).

That in itself is probably a virtue. Really prolonged exposure to the sun ages the skin and increases the incidence of skin cancer. Many dermatologists argue that any exposure beyond normal day-to-day activity is, on balance, unhealthy. From that perspective, the best suntan preparations are the ones with the most sunscreens. Of the very effective mixtures (and there aren't many), PreSun Lotion is the cheapest and least slimy.

T THE BEST TELEPHONE ANSWERING MACHINE

Telephone answering machines are even better than they sound. Not only do they answer the phone and record messages more cheaply and reliably than an answering service, but most allow you to monitor incoming calls and interrupt as you wish. Dynamite as protection against obscene calls and creditors.

Answering machines vary widely in price. The more you pay, the theory goes, the more durable the unit and the more versatile. No one has any statistics on comparative reliability, but the guarantees on the expensive machines are longer. The best of the stripped-down models is the Sanyo. It permits you to record an answering message of varying length, to monitor incoming calls (or shut off the monitoring speaker), and to keep a permanent record of the messages simply by replacing the standard tape cassette with a fresh one. Do-it-yourself installation is rather tricky with the Sanyo (and most others) unless your house is wired with plug-in telephone jacks. No matter how they are attached, Ma Bell won't like it. If she finds out, AT&T is legally entitled to an "installation" fee and a monthly tithe.

For a lot more money than the Sanyo, other machines provide some nice frills. Remote-control units allow you to call in and collect messages by activating the playback cycle with a high-frequency tone. Voice-actuated machines save the annoyance of listening to sixty seconds of silence after a hang-up. This, incidentally, is no small advantage—most people are unable to talk back to the box on the first try; others seem to object in principle. One machine, the Code-a-Phone, even allows you to keep a stock of three different answering messages on tap, rather than rerecord a new message as circumstances require.

THE BEST TELEVISION SHOW

Discipline is required here. Television has never been very good—and it probably averaged even worse in the Golden Age than it does today. Perry Mason's (the real Perry Mason's) brilliant weekly fifty-three-minute defense was no less formulaic ritual than Owen Marshall's brilliant weekly fifty-three-minute defense. *Racket Squad* and *Richard Diamond, Private Eye*, even *M Squad* and *Naked City*, were hopelessly naïve and unimaginative next to *Police Story* and *Hawaii Five-O*.

Granted, television drama is dead, but it was never really

alive. *Mama* ("My big brother Nels, my little sister Katrin
. . . but most of all I remember Mama") floated on a sea of
sentiment so saccharine that the Hanson family could have
made it through the panic of 1907 vending tears as molasses.
And who was ever convinced by John Beresford Tipton,
The Millionaire's ("Should you reveal where you got this
check to anyone but your wife [note sexism] you must return the unused portion") endlessly repeated message that
money couldn't buy happiness?

The grand experiments in theater-of-the-air—Playhouse
90, Goodyear Playhouse, Philco Playhouse, U.S. Steel Hour,
Kraft Theater—suffered the fatigue of small budgets and
weekly deadlines: for every *Requiem for a Heavyweight*,
Marty, or *Cyrano de Bergerac,* ten banal melodramas to
test the patience of a gin-sodden *Edge of Night* addict.

Fittingly, the best of television wasn't television at all,
but the last glories of vaudeville and radio comedy. Maybe
you didn't like Uncle Miltie in drag brushing off insults
from Arnold Stang—an acquired taste—but who could resist
Phil Silvers as Sergeant Bilko, the appropriately celebrated
Your Show of Shows (Sid Caesar, Imogene Coca, Carl
Reiner, Howie Morris), the dazzling, uncelebrated *Ernie
Kovacs Show,* Jackie Gleason's *Cavalcade of Stars* ("And
away we go"), Ed Wynn, Jack Benny, or Jimmy Durante?

Our—perhaps sentimental—choice is *Burns and Allen.*
George and Gracie started in vaudeville, moved to radio,
then fitted in perfectly to television of the fifties. Nominally
burdened by sitcom, they never permitted the flimsy stories
to get in the way of their awesome stand-up routines:
George, with comic timing equaled only by Jack Benny;
Gracie, the scatterbrain whose convoluted, overliteral logic

was at once funny and endearing—the schizophrenic root of comedy.

THE BEST TENNIS BALL

The seal of approval of the United States Lawn Tennis Association or the International Lawn Tennis Federation means almost nothing. It's not that the tennis associations are corrupt, it's simply that they are generally uncritical and occasionally arbitrary. Balls must not vary from the norm by more than $\frac{1}{16}$ inch in diameter, or $\frac{1}{32}$ ounce in weight, or about 4 percent in rebound. Sounds fine, but the trouble is, almost any conceivable tennis ball meets those undemanding criteria. Moreover, the USLTA/ILTF have nothing to say about how long a ball must meet the standards once it is in play, or how much the balls in any one can may differ from each other. The only balls that are automatically disqualified are the ones that come in colors, a useful innovation that ought to be encouraged.

There are two varieties of balls. The more common uses compressed air, as does a basketball, to generate a lively bounce. The newer pressureless tennis balls depend instead on rigid rubber covers for their rebound. In theory, the pressureless design is best, since balls under pressure tend to leak and wear out on the shelf after the can is opened (hence the desirability of storing open cans in the refrigerator). Pressureless balls also seem to resist wear from the constant friction with the court surface better, though there are some exceptionally durable high-pressure balls.

131

Among the pressureless variety, Tretorn and Dunlop are first-rate. Fine players will, however, note a certain leaden feel to either brand that will change the character of the game as dramatically as a switch from asphalt to clay. Great serves become merely good serves; overhead smashes are less devastating. Thus the tournament player with a fast modern game will be much happier with the best of the high-pressure balls—say, the Wright & Ditson or the Spalding Championship.

THE BEST TENNIS RACKET

It used to be easy to choose the best tennis racket. All rackets were made of wood; the better ones were manufactured from carefully cured lumber to resist warping, and then strung with gut by a dealer. Which one suited you depended on how strong you were. Flexible rackets put more power into your swing, but with a sacrifice of control. Stiffer rackets required more muscle to use, but gave you an extra margin for error. Generally, the most expensive rackets were the stiffest, though not always.

New technology changed all that. Racket frames are now also made from steel, aluminum, fiberglass, and combinations thereof. How much difference the new frames make is a matter of opinion. Metal rackets, in particular steel, do offer more power. For a tournament tennis player lacking only a big serve, metal can really make a difference. And proponents of the new rackets, not yet a majority, claim the extra power does not mean a sacrifice of control. The simple trade-offs inherent in wood, they argue, just don't apply.

One possible explanation for the difference is that the slimmer metal racket generates less wind resistance, so it takes less work to really get into the ball. That sounds fine, but traditionalists scoff at the notion that the minor advantage could make a noticeable difference. Another possibility is that the "sweet spot," the part of the racket that produces a clean hit and a satisfying plonk, is larger on the metal racket. An even more esoteric theory is that metal produces a more solid feel; vibrations from the collision between face and ball are more quickly damped, providing an edge of control at the split second of follow-through.

Our favorite is the Head Competition, an aluminum-fiberglass combination that provides the control characteristics of a very stiff racket, yet has more zing than wood. If you do choose metal, be prepared to pay. Good metal frames cost about twice as much as good wood frames and are unlikely to last as long. No one seems to have solved the problem of metal fatigue at the weld points; multi-ply wood does not share that difficulty.

Even if the metal frame does last, you are more likely to break a string with metal. Unless you pick one of the few metal rackets that protect the strings with plastic grommets or other devices, the constant metal/string friction will substantially reduce the time between eighteen-dollar restringing jobs. The problem is particularly acute for players who prefer natural gut stringing, the kind that provides the best feel and power.

Ten-speed bicycles aren't for everybody, though you would never know it from the sales. They are expensive—up to $600 for a production model—difficult to ride, and easy to damage. In city traffic you may find yourself, with a ten-pound anti-theft chain around your neck, shifting through seven or eight gears (one at a time) just to get up to cruising speed. Hit a pothole and you will bend a wheel ($15 plus). Even with the best of care you will need to service your ten-speed every few months. Figure $50 annually.

But if you aren't just anybody, the virtues of the ten-speed may propel you past *Consumer Reports* consciousness. With a ten-speed bicycle (and no other) a nonfanatic may look forward to easily pedaling forty miles of country road in five hours, all problems sublimated save the possibility of rain or truck traffic. With a ten-speed you can explore the châteaux of the Loire Valley in a week, as totally independent of the internal-combustion engine as the original occupants.

In essence, what you get for the money is a super-light bicycle frame—about fifteen pounds lighter than a sturdy Raleigh English Racer—and a set of gears that provide minutely graded choice over a rather narrow range. The virtues of light weight are self-evident, particularly if you plan to tour hilly country. And much of the investment in a fine bike goes into the seamless manganese-molybdenum steel tubular frame, which has been braised rather than welded for maximum strength. (Welding increases the probability of undetectable structural faults at the joints.)

All those gears don't give you a wider range to work with than a three-speed. But the more gears you have, the more likely that you will be able to maintain a steady pedal rhythm over varied terrain. As in long-distance swimming or running, a paced effort just short of the level that winds the athlete is most efficient. Ten-speeds use a derailleur mechanism that lifts the chain drive from sprocket to sprocket. Very clever, and very easy to mangle. The prudent bicyclist learns to repair his/her derailleur or takes along a mechanically adept friend.

Other accessories are relatively unimportant. The best brakes have cables attached to the calipers over the center of the wheel, not on the side. The best (read lightest) tires are tubeless "sew-ups"; for city use, plain old tube types are to be preferred because they are more rugged. The best pedals have toe straps. That way you can pull as well as push—every muscle counts.

Our choice for the best, the Peugeot U10 ($250), is several hundred dollars cheaper than the most expensive. But what you get for the extra bucks—a few more pounds shaved off the frame, a classy one-piece aluminum crank—just isn't worth it.

THE BEST THEORY OF THE ORIGIN OF THE UNIVERSE

The only theory for which there are even shreds of evidence is what George Gamov calls the Big Bang: a long (but measurable) time ago something made a dense ball of matter explode. Since no force was strong enough to contain the explosion, the universe has been expanding ever since. At some point, for reasons unexplained, clumps corresponding to star galaxies were formed, but the clumps were more or less evenly spread out through space. It follows, of course, that as the cloud of matter expands, the distance between galaxies also grows—to mix a metaphor, the spatial soup is getting thinner and thinner.

Here is where the evidence comes in. If the universe is expanding, the galaxies farthest away must be moving the fastest. There is no way to tell exactly how far away other galaxies are, but the brightness of the light and intensity of the other radiation they emit give us a fair idea—the closer they are, the stronger the signals.

Their speed can be inferred from the frequency of the radiation they emit. The faster they recede, the lower the frequency. The idea also works for ordinary sound waves. Stand near a super-highway and listen as a semi-trailer goes by. The pitch of the whine of the tires will drop just at the moment it passes. What's happening is easy to reconstruct. As the truck approaches, the pitch seems higher than it actually is, because the sound waves bunch up; as the truck moves away, the sound waves hitting your ear are spread out. In other words, their frequency is lower. So goes the analogous "Red Shift" for radiation in space. The degree to which light frequencies from receding galaxies are lower than would be expected gives us a handle on their speed.

Estimated distances and estimated speeds in fact match neatly. The dimmest (hence farthest) objects in the sky are also the reddest. If you swallow this much of the story the rest is easy. We know how far apart the galaxies are and how fast they're moving. Thus we know when the movement began. The estimated age of the universe, the moment of the Big Bang, is 12 billion years.

So far so good. The Big Bang doesn't tell us much (why

the explosion? why galaxies?) but at least what it does explain fits the facts. The now passé alternative, called the Steady State theory, was invented, not to reconcile hypothesis with observation, but to save physicists the trouble of remolding the rest of physics to fit the implications of the Big Bang. It seems (though, in fairness, it doesn't follow absolutely) that if the Big Bang is correct, some basic physical constants of the universe—like the constant relating the strength of a gravitational field to the mass of and distance between bodies—aren't constants at all. They are slowly changing. There's no practical implication to the notion—747's will still fly, the moon will stay in orbit. But a lot of fundamental physics would have to be rethought.

Steady State advocates accept the evidence supporting the Big Bang and offer none of their own, but simply deny there had to be a "beginning" when matter was densely packed in space. Instead they argue that new matter is trickling into existence all the time, enough to keep the soup at an even consistency. It wouldn't take all that much to do the trick—just one new atom of hydrogen for every 45 cubic meters (the volume of a VW Microbus) every hundred years.

Apart from the philosophical problems—why is it more attractive to toss out the idea that the quantity of matter is fixed than it is to jettison the constancy of those troublesome physical constants?—there are problems of evidence. If the Steady State theory is correct, if things have always been as they are today, there would be no logical explanation for the bunching of certain radiation sources, called quasars, at the periphery of the measurable universe. Quasars are peculiar, galaxy-like objects radiating unbelievable amounts of energy that must represent some stage in the evolution of matter. Whatever their cause, the Steady State would have them evenly mixed in space. They are not.

The real trouble with these theories is their dependence on the most speculative of speculations. It's like an archaeologist reconstructing a building from a single stone. But as difficult as the archaeologist's job is, at least he knows that buildings have shape, or for that matter, that bricks don't float in air . . .

THE BEST TRAIN RIDE

First, forget funiculars, Disneyland-variety private lines, and Nelson Rockefeller's favorite, the Long Island Railroad. If the best means speed and efficiency to you, try the 120-mph Tokyo-Osaka Bullet Train. For romantic souls, the Paris-Istanbul Orient Express is still operating, but these days don't expect to meet any Hitchcock characters on board. And bring along sandwiches; they misplaced the dining car in the third reel.

For the practical-minded, there's the luxurious, reservations-only TEE (Trans-Europ-Express), with its individual swivel armchairs, and its rail network more extensive than a Frankfort banker's investment portfolio. The TEE's hard-to-beat schedules (2 hours 20 minutes, Brussels to the Gare du Nord in Paris) prove that airplanes are dispensable.

If all you are looking for is scenery, take the Bergen-Oslo ride, the Cape Town to Johannesburg Blue Train, or the trip from Casablanca to Marrakech. Our personal favorite is the Corsican Railway, 150 kilometers of precipitously perched tracks that carry you over *Treasure of the Sierra*

Madre terrain in coaches that are the last word in very old-fashioned comfort. To quote the official French government guide: "The Corsican Railway links Ajaccio, Bastia and Calvi by a picturesque route. It is a veritable scenic railway, zigzagging up and down mountains, flying valleys on high viaducts, tunneling under peaks and passes. It represents an extraordinary feat of 19th century pioneer engineering. The trains are equipped with bars . . ."

THE BEST TROUT FISHING IN THE WORLD

Undoubtedly in New Zealand. The most famous areas are on North Island, near the resort town of Rotorua. Probably the very best fishing, though, is on the mountainous, underpopulated South Island. An American, Stockton Rush, operates a luxury hotel and fishing club called Takaro near Lake Te Anau. There, for a rather stiff fee, guides will show you places where eight-pound trout beg to be taken by amateurs.

U THE BEST UNDERRATED OPERA

First performed in 1791, and rarely there-
after, Mozart's *La clemenza di Tito* suffers
from static staging, difficult singing roles, and a libretto too
ludicrous to mention. It does, however, have an achingly
sweet duettino, the "Deh prendi un dolce amplesso" and a
dramatic aria of note, the "Parto, parto."

The worthy *Clemenza* has been recorded by the Vienna
State Opera on London, with Istvan Kertész as conductor.
Major parts are sung by Krenn, Berganza, Casula, Popp,
Fassbaender, Franc.

THE BEST UNDISCOVERED HOTEL IN PARIS

The Résidence du Bois is hardly the most splendid hotel in
this city of nineteenth-century luxury, but it may be the
most charming. The tiny Résidence is a converted bourgeois
town house located on a quiet side street a few hundred
yards from the Etoile. Each of the sixteen rooms is dis-
tinctively furnished, each has a view of the garden or the
interior courtyard. There is no restaurant, but the manage-

ment is prepared to serve meals *sur commande* in your room or by the garden.

If Paris does not mean the 16ᵉ Arrondisement to you, you may prefer the Relais Bisson, an inn with just a dozen rooms on the quai Grands-Augustins, opposite the Palais de Justice. The Relais is located above a famous restaurant of the same name, one that earned two Michelin stars in an era when stars were harder to come by. Today the restaurant has fallen from the *Guide*'s grace, but remains a favorite for its sophisticated St.-Germain clientele.

Most of the small, wallpapered, antique-furnished rooms overlook Notre Dame. Heavy wooden shutters lock out the sound of traffic at night on the quai, and save for the occasional shudder of the Orly rapid transit underneath and a mini-refrigerator in an alcove, one might feel Paris had not changed since the Third Republic.

THE BEST UNDISCOVERED HOTEL IN ROME

This once-seedy small hotel on the Via della Fontanella, not far from the Spanish Steps, has recently been renovated as a first-class hotel. The small rooms are quiet, unflashily modern, and air-conditioned. With luck, it will remain undiscovered. The management has to date been unwilling to cooperate with the *Guide Michelin* inspectors, and we are unwilling to give the name, so that it may remain undiscovered.

THE BEST UNDISCOVERED WINES

"Undiscovered" is a relative term when applied to wines. Back a few years, when the cost of a bottle of Château Palmer was less than a fifth of Dewar's, people used to "discover" $2.98 classified-growth Bordeaux that had previously been the closely guarded secret of 80,000 Frenchmen. But those days are gone forever, thanks to the virtually fixed supply of high-quality wine and the virtually limitless growth of the world market for status. It is no more likely that anyone will unearth a Burgundian slope whose product is indistinguishable from La Romanée-Conti than that Texaco will hit oil in the Bronx.

Still, some fine wines are more discovered than others. The most outrageously discovered are the twenty or thirty Bordeaux châteaux—from Lafite to Ausone—whose names tumble so easily from the lips of ad execs lunching on expense accounts. Somehow the ultimate Burgundies like Clos de Beze and La Tache have never quite made it in America, though there are enough British life peers knowledgeable in these matters to keep the prices out of sight. One's best hope for a bargain is to buck the trends in fashionability, since current wine prices only imperfectly reflect quality. A few possibilities:

Grand Cru Chablis. The elite among Chablis, these palegold wines (Blanchots, Les Clos, Grenouilles, Vaudesir, Valmur, Bougros, Les Preuses) are grown on just one third of a square mile of hillside a half hour's drive from Auxerre. They deserve to be rated among the finest white wines in the world—often as good as the more highly prized Corton-Charlemagne and Montrachet grown to the south—but popular taste has passed them by. This may be because

Chablis is so demanding of the palate—*Grand Cru* Chablis is uncompromisingly dry, and the very best (Les Clos) conceals a hint of the taste of steel.

Sauternes. In the nineteenth century no French wine was more highly esteemed than Château d'Yquem, the syrupy-sweet sauternes with a redeeming dash of acid in the after-taste. D'Yquem still fetches remarkable prices, but other sauternes almost its equal—notably Château Climens and Château Coutet—are still relatively cheap. Here there is no question why they are out of favor. Sauternes is too sweet to be drunk with most food—though certain hardy Victorian types used to down it with the fish course—and too easily confused by the uninitiated with myriad sweet, worthless peasant wines. No sugar is added to a true sauternes. The 16 percent alcohol and incredible sugar content come from letting the grapes dehydrate on the vine, victims of what the French call the noble rot. The result of this process is a concentration of flavor as well as sugar, and a subtlety worthy of very great wine.

Moselle and Rheingau. These are the best of the German wine districts that line the valleys of the Rhine and its tributaries. Within them are vineyards that produce white wines of the highest standard—Moselles like Wehlener Sonnenuhr, alive with fruit but capable of improvement with age; Rheingaus like Rauenthaler Baiken, with the characteristic flowery bouquet of the region toughened by a backdrop of Riesling grape. One reason they are so cheap is that a bit of expertise is required to pick out the good ones from run-of-the-mill German wine. Perhaps a more satisfying explanation is that the reputation of the region is based on the sweet, late-picked *Auslese* and *Trocken-beerenauslese* wines, which are made much like sauternes.

143

As a consequence, the relatively dry wines from the same estates sell for the price of miscellaneous shippers' blends of white Burgundies.

Chianti Classico. The miserable reputation of Italian wine is in part deserved. Laws governing the production of wine are new and have yet to be extended to cover many exports. Vineyards capable of fine wine are lost in the shuffle. Hence ordinary Chianti is usually the harsh red wine in a straw-covered bottle meant to be gulped with the lasagna. Its undebased hybrid, Chianti Classico, is a complex yet robust wine sold in Bordeaux-shaped bottles. Chianti Classico is, in general, a carefully made wine with an overpowering nose that can attain the quality of many lesser classified French wines. But thanks to the historic anarchical tendencies of Italian entrepreneurs, it's much, much cheaper.

V *THE BEST VICE-PRESIDENT*

The Constitution provides for succession in case the President dies, resigns, becomes incompetent, or is kicked out of office. And though the

Founding Fathers occasionally lapsed from infinite wisdom —it was the Constitutional Convention, after all, that decided a slave only counted as three fifths of a person—they did show the common sense to make sure the Presidency could not fall to some haberdasher or hack county executive without benefit of election. By Article II, the V.P. would be the runner-up candidate in the Electoral College.

Common sense wasn't quite good enough, for the system was doomed almost from the start. Electors had two votes to cast, but each had to go to a different candidate. In the first election Washington received everybody's first vote and John Adams was a distant second in a field of eleven. So far, so good; Washington dominated politics and his presence kept factions in their place.

But it doesn't take a graduate course in game theory or even much junior high student council experience to see where things would head once political power was more evenly split. In 1796 the Federalist Party caucus chose Adams for President and Thomas Pinckney from South Carolina for V.P. Since the Federalists won a majority of electors in the popular vote, a little party discipline would have given them both offices.

Alexander Hamilton had other ideas and secretly urged a group of Southern Federalists to dump Adams from their ballots. Hamilton expected the rest of the Federalist electors to vote the party line. Then Pinckney would end up on top and Adams second. Unfortunately for Hamilton, Adams's supporters cut Pinckney in greater numbers, enough to push the Southerner out of the running altogether. The Federalists ended up with an anti-Federalist V.P., Thomas Jefferson.

Four years later, the game got even more complicated. Anti-Federalist electors won big with a ticket of Jefferson and Aaron Burr. Remembering what had happened to Pinckney, Burr insisted the electors toe the line. The result, naturally, was a tie for first place. That gave the House of Representatives, which was still controlled by the Federalists, a shot at Jefferson. The majority in the House was under no obligation to ratify the anti-Federalists' choice and in fact tried to make a deal with Burr (shades of George Wallace) that would have cost Jefferson the Presidency. When Burr declined, the Federalists decided on the thirty-sixth ballot to go along with Jefferson's popular mandate.

Nobody wanted to go through that again. Some enterprising young Herman Kahn might have figured out a way of getting himself elected with two thirds of the support of the Rhode Island delegation. One solution would have been to limit each elector to one vote. But that would have made the opposition candidate the Vice-President and built in an extra incentive for assassination. Instead, the Twelfth Amendment required electors to cast separate ballots for President and Vice-President. This put the nomination safely within the control of the party leadership, and the second office, of course, declined.

Adams, Jefferson, and Burr were followed by the likes of:

Richard M. Johnson (1837–41), whose chief claim to fame was the killing of Tecumseh in the War of 1812. Johnson otherwise distinguished himself by moonlighting as an innkeeper in suburban Washington and selling his black mistress after she tried to run away with an Indian.

Schuyler Colfax (1869–73), who was caught, along with half the Congress, holding stock in Crédit Mobilier, a corporation formed to milk federal grants intended for the construction of the Union Pacific Railroad. Colfax recollected later that he bought the stock with a $1,000 bill that had arrived in the mail from an unknown admirer.

Henry Wilson (1873–75), who for some mysterious reason changed his name from Jeremiah J. Colbath. J.J. turns out also to not have been above a little Crédit Mobilier baksheesh.

They certainly haven't all been such ideal candidates for the Roman Hruska Supreme Court seat. Teddy Roosevelt and Henry Wallace were political figures in their own right; John C. Calhoun, Martin Van Buren, and Harry Truman, at least zircons in the rough. However, our volume requires a choice in keeping with the high purposes of the office, the kind of man who has helped make the nation what it is today. For this reason we might have turned to William Almon Wheeler (1877–81), whose nomination inspired his running mate, Rutherford B. Hayes, to ask, "Who is Wheeler?" but instead we have settled upon William Rufus Devane King. Not only did he have the most formidable middle names of any V.P., but he also had the least blemished record of service. Mr. King was administered the oath of office in March 1853. He did not survive a month.

THE BEST VIOLIN

The greatest violins were made in the northern Italian city of Cremona between 1600 and 1750, the creations of three craftsmen—Nicolò Amati, Antonio Stradivari, and Giuseppe

Antonio Guarneri del Gesù. No one since has been able to produce instruments of comparable quality, though it is difficult to say why. There are no technical mysteries to be overcome: violin engineering is better understood now than it was in the eighteenth century; all the raw materials—woods, varnishes—used in Cremona are still available. Besides, the violin is not some sort of infinitely delicate flower for which tolerances of one ten-thousandth of an inch matter; great instruments vary considerably in design and materials. Possibly the only missing ingredient is time. Violins unquestionably mature over decades. Perhaps the refinement process goes on for hundreds of years.

Of the three masters, Amati is least in fashion. His violins are delicate and pure, instruments better suited to chamber music than orchestral. In contrast, Guarneri violins are bold and powerful in tone, the sound more passionate than intellectual. Stradivariuses range somewhere in between, though some would claim they simply dominate the Amatis. Oistrakh, Milstein, and Menuhin play Stradivariuses; Heifetz, Stern, and Szeryng play Guarneris. The Stradivariuses are surely more versatile and easier to master—many professionals who prefer the Guarneri effect own Stradivariuses, but rarely the other way around. Comparisons are also complicated by the idiosyncrasies of individual violins. Guarneri made mediocre instruments, the so-called prison violins, as well as great ones. And while Stradivariuses never deviate from a very high standard, there are considerable variations among them; early Stradivariuses are more like Amatis.

By the test of the marketplace—a dubious test for an era in which a Velázquez oil can fetch $5.5 million—Stradivariuses are most highly prized. The "Lady Anne Blunt" Stradivarius was auctioned at Sotheby's in 1971 for $200,-000. The more famous "Dolphin" Stradivarius was sold by Jascha Heifetz for less than half that much as recently as 1967. Sheer scarcity may ultimately drive the price of Guarneris even higher—there are probably only 150 in existence, to 1,200 Stradivariuses, and many of them are the inferior products of his youth.

THE BEST WAY TO ASSESS PROPERTY TAXES

Every kid knows that the best way to split a piece of cake is to have first choice after the other kid cuts it. Similarly, you can finesse incentives to cheat on property taxes by allowing the owner to assess his own, but require him to sell the property at the assessed value to anyone who wants it.

A variation on the same theme is used to keep first-class thoroughbreds from picking up easy prize money against lesser horseflesh. In a claiming event—say a $10,000 claiming race—the horses are for sale after the race for $10,000.

THE BEST WAY TO AVOID JET LAG

The fatigue and disorientation that follow a flight to Europe aren't merely the product of a sleepless night cooped up with 350 members of your affinity group, or the premixed martini and glorified TV dinner. Body rhythms, the chemical changes regulated by hormone output, are rigidly keyed to a twenty-four-hour cycle. If you disrupt the cycle, you pay. The sun tells you it is morning, but your hormones tell you it is 2 a.m. Complete biological adaptation takes more than a week.

The best strategy for minimizing the impact of the inevitable trauma is to anticipate the effect and begin the transition as soon as possible. Meals are a crucial cue to the timing mechanism. Don't reinforce the old rhythm by eating at the old mealtimes. Eat little or nothing. Try to nap on the airplane and then avoid sleep in Europe until the sun sets.

Best of all, schedule a daylight flight, a luxury reluctantly offered by a half-dozen airlines on the competitive North Atlantic run. Get up a few hours early before departing and go to bed a few hours late (local time) on arrival. If you are young and adaptable you may feel no malaise whatsoever. If you are not, the curse will pass in a day or two.

THE BEST WAY TO BECOME VERY RICH

We mean very rich, not rich. A million dollars hardly qualifies—any ob.-gyn. worthy of his Mass. General residency, or lawyer attuned to the hustle in divorce court, can accumulate that much in twenty years. Real money, the kind that gets you an oceanfront estate in Palm Beach and a Vermeer for the dining room, isn't just the happy reward for hard work.

Method No. 1: Inherit It.

Well, obviously, but, as they say in the White House, it is not an operative concept. In spite of a federal inheritance tax with a 77 percent bite in the $10 million bracket, fortunes can still be passed along nearly intact through gifts and trusts. Inheritance may not build character, but it does economize on ulcers. Heirs or trust-fund beneficiaries in the $100-million-plus category include no less than eight Mellons (the children of Richard King Mellon and Sarah Mellon Scaife) and six Hunts (the children of H. L. Hunt); four Gettys have trusts worth some $30 million each, but they are going to have to wait for control of the $2 to $4 billion mother lode.

Method No. 2: Monopolize Something Important.

This is the classic way, though the opportunities have shrunk of late. Most of the great American fortunes were made by gaining control of an industry and enlisting government support—regulatory commissions, protective tariffs, subsidy programs—against potential intruders. Of the sixty-six individuals with assets over $150 million on *Fortune* magazine's 1968 list, eighteen owe their wealth to the oil business, six to chemicals and mining, six to banking and insurance, four to automobiles, three to drugs, and two to railroads.

Method No. 3: Invent Something Important, Manufacture It Yourself, and Hang on to the Stock.

Broadly interpreted, this is the romantic American way. Dr. Edwin H. Land turned self-developing film into $500

151

million in Polaroid stock. Chester Carlson parlayed the first successful dry photocopier into a couple million shares of Xerox.

Less celebrated good ideas also work nicely. Roy J. Carver purchased the rights to a superior tire-retreading process used in Germany, improved on it, and became the largest manufacturer of retreads in the world. His stock in Bandag, Inc., is worth about $300 million. Vernon Krieble's Loctite— a sealant that hardens without exposure to the air, yet is simple to use—has made his family about $100 million. Dozens of other inventions might also have qualified, but either the inventors were working for somebody else, or they took their royalties and ran.

Method No. 4: Shake up a Sleepy Industry.

Ray Kroc busted the fifties image of the drive-in as teenage hangout and replaced it with Ronald McDonald, the Big Mac, tough franchising standards, and polite, part-time student labor exempt from the minimum-wage laws. Jack Eckerd discovered the perfect prescription for his retail drug business (three hundred stores) in Florida's geriatrics belt: rock-bottom drug prices, not-so-rock-bottom cosmetics prices, and fundamentalist religion/politics. The insight that lonely suburban housewives would do almost anything for company made $300 million for Edna McConnell, president of Avon Products, which was the hottest stock of the sixties.

But no industry is quite as fat and contented as insurance, and no industry has spawned so many fresh multimillionaires. One way to beat the old-line giants was to bypass the friendly, inefficient neighborhood insurance agent. Leonard Davis, the founder of the Penn Colonial Group, and Leo

Goodwin of GEICO capitalized discount operations into personal fortunes over $100 million; Arthur DeMoss of the National Liberty Corporation peddled policies directly by mail. Another way was to insure something new—Edward Frey and Richard Riebel (Centennial Corp.) covered mobile homes; Max Karl (MGIC) guaranteed mortgages.

THE BEST WAY TO PLAY MONOPOLY

In a standard game of Monopoly, everything depends on who lands on the good properties first. Almost any property is a bargain at the list price—players have even been known to do well on Water Works and Electric Company, and the railroads are a positive bonanza.

It's a different game entirely if you just change one rule: when a player lands on an unowned property, put it up for open auction rather than let him buy it at list price from the bank. Bidding removes most of the luck from the game, leaving just enough chance to let you alibi your loss to your nine-year-old kid.

When players have to bid against each other for property, they quickly become short on cash. Properties that were worth far more than list price in an ordinary game are now, paradoxically, sometimes worth less. Take North Carolina, for example, at a $300 list. Normally you'd snap it up rather than be left heavy on cash and short on monopolies. But in a bidding game, you'll have to consider the fact that houses on the greens cost $200 each. Before you could hit the opposition for a single $390 landing rental, you would have to build two houses on each green for a total cost of $1,200, on top of what you've paid for the properties. Money like that just isn't around in the bidding game, and it makes sense to buy up humbler lots—especially the light blues, where a $750 investment in improvements buys hotels with a $550 or $600 (for Connecticut) landing rental.

THE BEST WAY TO REDUCE AIRPORT CONGESTION

The scenario: it is a Friday evening in late August. You and three hundred other unfortunates are imprisoned on a 747, circling O'Hare. Stacked up along with your jumbo are two dozen commercial flights, each filled to what the airlines euphemistically call capacity—four thousand slightly claustrophobic souls longing to be released from their misery. Barring emergencies, the rule of the runway is first come, first served; and first at this moment is a twin-engine Beechcraft carrying three executives back from a sales pitch in Racine, Wisconsin, less than a hundred miles away. The Beechcraft makes a slow, safe approach to the main runway, thereby adding two minutes' waiting time for the twenty-five jets up above.

The cost of those two minutes conservatively averages $10 per plane in fuel, wear and tear, and salaries, about $250 for the whole flock. Surely the passengers value their wasted time at ten cents a minute—another $800. So the real cost of landing the Beechcraft at O'Hare this Friday

154

evening is over $1,000, not counting its share for the use of the multimillion-dollar air traffic control equipment and the time of dozens of tower personnel on hand. Untroubled by such calculations, indeed unaware that such calculations could be made, the pilot of the Beechcraft arranges to pay a landing fee of about $10 before leaving the terminal.

A cynic might suspect that this preposterous situation could not last long unless somebody important benefited. A cynic would be right. The sensible solution would be to charge planes what the service really costs—the time of the other users, plus a bit to pay for the landing. That might amount to $1,000 to use O'Hare's sophisticated system at prime time, but only $5 for landing in New Haven on a Saturday afternoon. When the big New York airports went partway with a $25 minimum, 30 percent of the private planes at LaGuardia found the price too steep and cleared the space for jets.

Why, then, haven't the airlines, the major victims of crowding, pushed for rational pricing elsewhere? They are trapped by their own greed. Today almost all the cost of running airports is borne by taxpayers (the Federal Aviation Agency foots the bill for safety equipment) and by airport concessionaires (ask Avis how much rent it pays for those cute little booths). Landing fees just cover any expenses left over and are usually figured by the weight of the airplanes. A few years ago, O'Hare charged about $40 for a DC-9 and about $5 for a Beechcraft King Air.

Most of the airlines are simply afraid that discussion of revising the tariffs will give somebody the bright idea of using them to pay for airports or, heaven forbid, as additional revenue sources for municipalities. Instead they grin

155

and bear it, or lobby for the best airports tax money can buy so there is elbow room for everybody.

THE BEST WAY TO STAY ALIVE

The life expectancy of an American male born today is about sixty-seven years. If he makes it over the actuarial hump of infant mortality (not a very big hump for the sons of the middle classes born in hospitals), that figure goes up to sixty-nine years. At age forty-five, assuming the statistics don't change dramatically, he will have passed through a prime heart attack period and can expect to make it to seventy-two. By comparison, his grandfather born in 1900 had only a fifty-fifty chance of reaching forty-seven. That's progress.

Well, yes and no. Almost all of the improvement has come from public health measures—water systems safe from sewage, fresh food storage—and a few big advances in the treatment of bacterial infections. Americans are far less likely to be knocked off in the prime of life by smallpox or tuberculosis. Routine virus diseases or body wounds rarely lead to death any more, given the ability of antibiotics and sulfa drugs to control secondary infections.

But for all the billions spent on more specialized forms of treatment, we have hardly made a dent in mortality from major degenerative processes, the progressive diminishment of capacity of the vital organs and the diseases that push them down the road—arteriosclerosis, cancer, kidney disease. Those lucky enough to reach sixty-five in 1900 had

156

an even shot of living to seventy-eight; in spite of the best efforts of the medical establishment, a sixty-five-year-old today is unlikely to make it past eighty. And chances are the last few thousand happy days will be plagued by some combination of arthritis, incontinence, blindness, and mental incompetence.

There seem two avenues of escape. The first is clean living. Virtually everything that is pleasant to ingest or can cause stress speeds aging. Cholesterol-laden animal fats harden and narrow the arteries, increasing the risk of clotting and cutting down the blood supply to the brain and kidneys. Just plain overeating strains the circulatory system and may cause diabetes, a disease that, untreated, pounds away at the vital organs. Smoking progressively destroys the capacity of the lungs to exchange carbon dioxide and oxygen, overworks the heart through constriction of blood vessels, and, of course, raises the probability of cancer. Excessive alcohol scars the liver and stomach lining, weakens the heart muscle, and damages brain tissue. Mental stress in some unknown way raises blood pressure, which, in turn, threatens virtually every vital organ.

That humans can survive decades longer under ideal conditions, there is little question. Consider the village of Vilcabamba in one of the isolated upland valleys of Ecuador. What we would call poverty keeps the consumption of expensive animal fats to a minimum, caloric intake below North American levels, and workdays long. Family life appears to be stable; no special forms of insecurity threaten the individual. Retirement in old age is unheard of. The temperate climate, clean water supply, and isolation protect the town from standard health menaces or the infiltration of alien genetic weaknesses. More than 10 percent of the population of this cardiologist's paradise are over seventy (6 percent in the United States), about 1 percent are over one hundred (U.S., 0.1 percent), suggesting an average life-span well into the eighties.

A much larger protected bubble of longevity, Abkhazia (a republic within the USSR) doesn't fit so neatly—the citizens eat plenty of animal fat. But the rest of the pattern is there: low-calorie diet, plenty of hard physical labor, continuing work, and respect for old people.

Staying calm, skinny, well-exercised, useful, and uncorrupted by future shock may get you a long way, but the race against death—even in Swiss clinics—is never won. Free of disease, the body still wears out after about 110 years. Just why is a matter of some controversy. One school of thought lays the blame to the failure of life-preserving systems within the body—subtle hormone changes, or the collective weight of years of wastes from cell activity that interfere with vital functions. These in turn throw big hormone systems out of kilter, limit the ability of cells to regenerate tissue, or invite disease by weakening the immune system.

The other view focuses on the finite capacity of cells to reproduce. A human cell isolated from the organism will cease to divide after a time on its own. At the crux of that failure is the role of the genetic matrix that "remembers" cell function and makeup over generations. Perhaps reproduction chemically fixes the ability of the genetic material to survive. Just as likely, the DNA molecular memory is randomly damaged over time; occasional errors creep into succeeding generations, eventually limiting the capacity to divide. Since the body depends on the reproduction of billions of cells, the random pattern of errors may create certain disaster—the same sort of statistical certainty that ensures the house will win at roulette.

Neither theory contains the glimmering of a cure for old age. But then, neither do they suggest that mortality may not be remediable. The search is at an incredibly primitive stage because biochemists and biophysicists have hardly begun to flesh out the skeleton of the life sciences. Medical research until very recently was only a collection of sophisticated guesses and slowly accumulated trial-and-error lessons about things comprehended not at all—a profitable exercise, but one that can promise no reward for systematic effort. Possibly some chemical therapy can curb the suicidal urges of cells once the urge is understood, or possibly fresh genetic material can be introduced to rejuvenate cell reproduction.

Of course, there is no reason to expect solutions that mimic triumphs of the past. If the organs of the body must wear out, why not replace them? Transplants or artificial-organ substitutions, as routine as they might become, cannot be the answer—eventually the whole mechanism must fail: skin, muscle tissue, brain, nerves. But it may be possible to finesse the whole problem by growing whole new bodies, twins identical to the originals save for memory, from the genetic information contained within single cells. If it also becomes possible to copy and implant memory, there is no reason to suppose that a person could not carry on indefinitely, periodically switching to younger, healthier

159

bodies. Who knows, we might have Richard Nixon to kick around forever.

THE BEST WAY TO STOP SMOKING

The most successful technique is to associate smoking with unpleasant sensations—in psychology jargon, aversive conditioning. The idea is simple. Each time the smoker takes a drag, a machine blows a puff back in his face. After a few sessions a whiff of smoke or even the idea of smoking causes nausea. And the nausea seems to last. A University of Oregon research group found that 60 percent of an admittedly well-motivated sample of volunteers were able to remain off the weed for at least six months.

Anyone can try a crude version of anti-tobacco conditioning. Just double or triple your normal habit for a few days, or until you feel really awful. Then stop altogether.

Other kinds of anti-smoking reinforcement have a poor, or at least poorly documented, chance of success. Group therapy—Alcoholics Anonymous style—seems to work, but recidivism rates are high. The same pattern is evident in drama-therapy sessions in which smokers act out their own deaths from lung cancer. But this shouldn't be surprising in view of how much positive reinforcement day-to-day smoking brings—every puff a small drama of tension and relief.

Over-the-counter drugs to prevent smoking seem to produce minor successes. Here it is likely that the pills act as a placebo—a psychological crutch to individual will. Of course, there is nothing wrong with placebos. Dumbo flew with a magic feather; hospital patients seem to do about as well on sugar pills as on codeine, providing they don't know about the switch.

The usual way people quit smoking is just to stop. However, nicotine may be physically addicting—i.e., stopping may cause physical withdrawal symptoms, as alcohol or heroin do. And on that rationale many try to give it up slowly. Leonid Brezhnev has a cigarette case with a time lock that releases only once an hour. For emergencies, or perhaps owing to lack of faith in Soviet technology, he also carries a regular pack.

But the approach is at best dubious. Physical withdrawal symptoms from nicotine are minor, if they exist at all. What really must be conquered is the psychological dependence. Moreover, a gradual cutback makes every remaining cigarette more pleasurable. Anyone with the constitution to stand gradual withdrawal certainly has the willpower to go cold turkey.

THE BEST WAY TO SURVIVE IN THE COLD

No matter what Sergeant Preston or his dog King had to say about it, subzero-weather survival is a matter of common sense. The idea is to conserve heat. Keep moving and you only expose a greater surface to the elements and waste the thin layer of warm air that forms around your body. Alcohol kills the pain, but it also dilates blood vessels near the skin, dumping more calories into the atmosphere.

Sleep—yes, sleep—is the most efficient heat conservation mode. Find or make a shelter—a cave, a lean-to, a house of snow—curl up in a ball, and go to sleep.

THE BEST WEIGHT ATTAINED BY THE LATE AGA KHAN III FOR HIS PERIODIC WEIGHINGS

243½ pounds in 1946, when he was presented with his weight in diamonds. For gold and platinum weighings he was considerably slimmer.

THE BEST WINE VINTAGE OF
THE CENTURY

Apart from the small percentage of wine grown in temperate climates—mostly in France and Germany—vintages are almost meaningless. Italian, Spanish, and California wine grapes receive the dubious benefits of predictably mild, rainy winters and intensely sunny summers. That precludes the kind of disaster that turned the 1968 Bordeaux to dishwater, but limits the potential of the finished wine. Besides, outside France and Germany, the labeling laws can at times be stretched. In many parts of Portugal the clocks stopped in 1961. One wonders what they have done with the grape crop since. In Hungary the state wine monopoly's alternate road to socialism leads only to 1964.

Other problems: weather is not uniform within a wine region, and neither is the skill or luck of individual vintners. Hence there is probably more variation in quality among well-known wines of the same vintage (particularly in a marginal year like 1957) than between decent vintage years.

To add to the confusion, prestige wines are a very big business. Millions of dollars ride on the accuracy of predictions of vintage quality. White wines can be judged quickly after they are made, usually a year or two later. Only really unusual whites—the finest of the German *Auslese*, the regal *Grands Crus* of the Côte d'Or—have any chance of improving in the bottle. But all good red Bordeaux and a fair proportion of red Burgundies take five to twenty years to peak after bottling. A prediction in 1973 about the quality of 1971 Château Haut-Brion is nothing more than an educated guess.

163

Once the major shippers are committed to a vintage, however, those educated guesses have a way of dominating the clubby wine media. The huge 1959 vintage was willed to be the vintage of the century, God's first fat year after three lean ones. Cases of the First Great Growth Bordeaux were traded like computer software stocks in the mid-sixties; the retail price of Lafite hit $80 a bottle. Only in the last two or three years has the truth dribbled out: 1959 is a B+ vintage; the wines are soft and rapidly maturing, quite similar to and little better than the unheralded '62's.

However risky it may be, the rating game is still amusing. Of the prewar vintages in red Bordeaux and Burgundy only '28 and '29 are outstanding, though Lafite failed in both. Trying to compare these years with contemporary vintages is like comparing Babe Ruth with Hank Aaron. No prewar vintage is still near its peak today. Of the postwar vintages, the real competition is among '45, '47, and '61. '47 was an astounding year in Burgundy, a mixed success in Bordeaux. The wines of St.-Emilion are the best ever; the Médocs are not in the same class.

If one is to believe the opinion-makers, '61 tops the field —surely two dozen or so of the lesser '61 Bordeaux dominate the First Great Growths of an average year. But the key to the popular success of the '61's is that they matured quickly. A fifth-growth château like Lynch-Bages was ready to drink in 1968. The '45's were untouchable until the 1960's and are just now hitting their prime. They may never be bettered.

THE BEST WORLD WAR I GENERAL

Choosing the best commander in the Great War is a bit like selecting the most honest member of the Harding Administration or the ablest pilot in the Cambodian Air Force.

Surely von Moltke, Germany's first wartime chief of staff and reluctant inheritor of Count Schlieffen's battle plan, merits a mention. The general didn't do so badly, considering the odds. He stayed afloat in a sea of megalomaniacs, the courtiers and Prussian woodenheads who believed Germany could defeat the combined armies of Britain, France, and Russia with only the Hapsburgs as allies. The Schlieffen Plan, signed and sealed in 1905, called for an end run around the French army through Belgium, then encirclement of Paris, and finally an assault on the French forces cut off from their supplies.

Von Moltke almost made it. But Schlieffen designed without margin for error; it was, after all, a plan for defeating an army of equal size. Von Moltke made errors: a few days too many tramping through Belgium, a few missed opportunities on the battlefield, a few logistic failures. The army ran out of initiative and energy at the Marne and von Moltke lost the chance to end the war in 1914. Close, but no cigar.

The French commander at the Marne, General Joffre, played the stubborn peasant to von Moltke's rigid aristocrat. Joffre's only accomplishment, save lining up a million men at the Marne, was to relieve the French nation of any threat from the population explosion. In the opening days of the war his counteroffensives—deliberately aimed at the most heavily fortified German positions—accounted for the first few hundred thousand French casualties and the first few square miles of Alsace-Lorraine to be liberated. The best was to come: 315,000 dead at the strategically worthless fort of Verdun, 200,000 more at the festivities on the Somme.

Not ones to shirk a challenge, the commanders of the British Army, Sir John French and later Sir Douglas Haig, conducted equally decisive experiments on the relative durability of human flesh and machine-gun bullets. The results: 420,000 dead patriots at the Somme (60,000 on a single day, the record), 300,000 in the three-foot-deep mud of Passchendaele.

If we must eliminate these worthy artisans of the attrition strategy from contention, what of commanders more inclined to measure success in miles rather than bodies? General Brusilov's three-week southern campaign utterly destroyed the enemy; but his victory shouldn't really be counted, since the enemy was only the imperial Austrian Army and the Russians themselves absorbed one million casualties.

General Ludendorff's virtues as a soldier are less tarnished, and some would be inclined to honor him for it. As the real brains and nerve of the German campaign in the East in 1914, he supervised the dismemberment of the Russian Army at Tannenberg. However, Ludendorff was also a politician and he, as much as anyone else, was responsible for passing by the chances for a compromise peace. First in 1916, when Tsar Nicholas offered to call it a draw if the Germans withdrew to Poland. Later, in 1918, when Ludendorff risked the last major Western offensive, lost, and then surrendered to President Wilson in pique.

By elimination, that leaves Foch, the nasty little tyrant

of the French general staff. General Foch blundered into
the stalemate of trench warfare as innocently as everyone
else. As an army commander at the Somme he tossed away
200,000 lives in 1915–16, then sulked when public opinion
saved the rest of his corps from the slaughter. But Foch,
unlike every other Allied commander, over the years
learned to come in out of the rain and had the personality
to resist dullards like Haig who insisted on getting wet.
Promoted over Marshal ("They shall not pass") Pétain—
the dimmest mind to lead troops in the war—Foch effec-
tively controlled the Allies during the German offensive of
1918. Instead of digging in, he withheld his reserves and
retreated. Ludendorff pushed on and eventually stumbled,
victim to the same technologically inspired inertia that had
spoiled every offensive since von Moltke's.

Z THE BEST ZOO

Pressed to comment on the Victorians' en-
thusiasm for the newly created London Zoo,
the historian Macaulay protested, "I have seen the Hippo
both asleep and awake, and I can assure you that, asleep or
awake, he is the ugliest of the Works of God."

Americans apparently don't agree. Once the poorest step-
children of city government, rivaled only by libraries, zoos
are so popular that beer companies and movie-studios-
turned-conglomerates are rushing to build their own. The

Walt Disney Corporation even has plans to add a flesh-and-blood Wild Kingdom to its Orlando extravaganza. The true zoo head will claim that the United States has at least a dozen fine zoos, already. San Diego, the most famous, boasts a great collection of animals and a lush new 1,800-acre wild animal park in the suburbs, complete with monorail. Chicago's Brookfield is less elaborate, but houses a functioning wolf pack instead of the usual mangy individual specimens; Washington has two pandas, Nixon booty from his Opening to the Left. A private zoo, the Arizona–Sonora Desert Museum, provides air-conditioned underground views of its small collection that get you as close to desert life as you can ever hope to be. And what will someday be the best zoo in America, the well-heeled Bronx Zoo, contains a stunning World of Darkness in which usually shy night creatures come alive.

But none really compares with the Milwaukee County Zoo. Its main virtue is that it was started from scratch just twenty years ago—the 1950's site of the old zoo was victim to an Interstate highway. Every possible effort has been made to display animals in natural settings, a technique that is increasingly common, but nowhere else in so dedicated a fashion. Instead of cages, there are plains and rain forests—predators and prey are separated only by discreet moats. Where the illusion of nature isn't possible, glass has replaced bars; imaginative fiberglass landscaping, the traditional eighteenth-century insane-asylum style. It's even worth a visit in the winter—if only to see Siberian tigers taking dips in their half-frozen pool.

THE BEST OF THE BEST

& The Best Strategy for Investing in the Stock Market has a nice punch—informative, yet witty. Unfortunately the style is derivative. The Best Sports Car under $7,000 and the Best Stereo for $1,000 show remarkable taste, not to mention true commitment to *l'esthétique de la technologie*.

Of course, such devotion to materialism might be a bit much, were we to ignore matters of redeeming social significance—the Best Example of Military Logic, the Best Way to Reduce Airport Congestion—or fail to reveal a healthy (so we like to think) streak of cynicism: the Best World War I General, the Best Illustration of the "Convergence Theory" . . .

Alas, as you might have guessed, modesty prevents . . .

ACKNOWLEDGMENTS

Thank you to Nancy Bekavac, Ana Calvo, Guillermo Calvo, Leonard Chazen, Elaine Chubb, Anna Cosman, Don Cutler, Andrew Dalsimer, Kathy Dalsimer, Jill Danzig, John Daum, Michael Degener, Bill Finkle, Pamela Franklin, David Garth, Charles Gerson, Mary Joan Gerson, Rob Goble, Wendy Goble, Jeff Greenfield, Mary Benét Hale, Barbara Heyns, Caroline Isber, Roger Jellinek, David Kendall, Si Lazarus, John Lee, Linda Lee, Susan Lee, Mike Levine, Bonnie Mathieson, Don Mathieson, Wendy Moonan, Victor Navasky, Barbara Neilson, Anne Passell, Nick Passell, Rhoma Paul, David Previant, Lois Previant, Peter Reuter, Peter Schliesser, David Schwartz, Elisabeth Sifton, Helen Whitney, Seymour Wishman, Helen Zottoli.